Experience the Magic and Ritual of the Seasons

Whether you are a newcomer to the Craft or found your way back many years ago, *Wheel of the Year* will be an important addition to your practical magic library. It is filled with magic and ritual for every day of your life and will enhance any system of Pagan ritual.

The Wheel of the Year turns slowly. Each day brings its own special rituals in accordance with the seasons. The magic and ritual of each day, no matter how slight, brings us new opportunities to align ourselves with the flow of creative energy in the universe.

Wheel of the Year discusses the major Sabbats, but the emphasis is on practical magic and rituals for those days and weeks between the Sabbats. This book also includes brief histories of many magical practices so that you can elaborate on or create rituals that have roots in ancient tradition.

The wealth of seasonal rituals and charms contained in *Wheel of the Year* are all easily performed with materials readily available, and they are simple and concise enough that the practitioner can easily adapt them to work within the framework of Pagan tradition.

- Learn when the best time is to gather materials for making a besom or Witches' Broom, and how to really use one.

- Learn the charms and rituals and the making of magical tools that coincide with the nesting season of migratory birds.

- Learn when the best time is to visit a faery forest or sacred spring, and what to do when you get there.

- Learn when the best time is to make a magic wand and why.

- Learn the secret Pagan symbolism of Christmas tree ornaments.

These and many other magical subjects are covered on a month-by-month basis, and the Table of Contents lists rituals, charms, and spells for each month, making this an invaluable reference book that is fast and easy to use. For Wiccans and Pagans of all traditions, *Wheel of the Year* can bring the joy and fulfillment of living the magical life.

About the Author

Pauline Campanelli and her husband Dan have been practicing Wiccans for 20 years. Because of their deep religious beliefs, they have evolved a lifestyle based on natural magic, and in their 18th-century home in western New Jersey, magic is a part of their everyday life.

Pauline has contributed articles on Pagan symbolism and traditions to *Circle Network News,* and *Fate* magazine has published her articles on personal experiences with the spirit world. Other paranormal experiences shared by Pauline and Dan have been included in Alan Vaughn's *Incredible Coincidence* and are on file at the University of Virginia.

Both Dan and Pauline are professional fine artists. Dan works in watercolors, Pauline in oils. They are each listed in 13 reference books, including *Who's Who in American Art* and *The International Dictionary of Biographies.* Their home and artwork have been featured in *Colonial Homes* and *Country Living* magazines, and New Jersey Network produced a television program on their artwork and lifestyle for PBS in 1985. Their paintings have been published as fine art prints that are available throughout the United States and Europe.

To Write to the Author

We cannot guarantee that every letter written to the author can be answered, but all will be forwarded. Both the author and the publisher appreciate hearing from readers, learning of your enjoyment and benefit from this book. Llewellyn also publishes a bi-monthly news magazine with news and reviews of practical esoteric studies and articles helpful to the student, and some readers' questions and comments to the author may be answered through this magazine's columns if permission to do so is included in the original letter. The author sometimes participates in seminars and workshops, and dates and places are announced in *The Llewellyn New Times.* To write to the author, or to ask a question, write to:

Pauline Campanelli
c/o THE LLEWELLYN NEW TIMES
P.O. Box 64383-091, St. Paul, MN 55164-0383, U.S.A.
Please enclose a self-addressed, stamped envelope for reply, or $1.00 to cover costs.

About Llewellyn's Practical Magick Series

To some people, the idea that "Magick" is *practical* comes as a surprise.

It shouldn't. The entire basis for Magick is to exercise influence over one's environment. While Magick is also, and properly so, concerned with spiritual growth and psychological transformation, even the spiritual life must rest firmly on material foundations.

The material world and the psychic are intertwined, and it is this very fact that establishes the Magickal Link: that the psychic can as easily influence the material as vice versa.

Magick can, and should, be used in one's daily life for better living! Each of us has been given Mind and Body, and surely we are under Spiritual obligation to make full usage of these wonderful gifts. Mind and Body work together, and Magick is simply the extension of this interaction into dimensions beyond the limits normally conceived. That's why we commonly talk of the "super-normal" in connection with domain of Magick.

The Body is alive, and all Life is an expression of the Divine. There is god-power in the Body and in the Earth, just as there is in Mind and Spirit. With Love and Will, we use Mind to link these aspects of Divinity together to bring about change.

With Magick we increase the flow of Divinity in our lives and in the world around us. We add to the beauty of it all—for to work Magick we must work in harmony with the Laws of Nature and of the Psyche. *Magick is the flowering of the Human Potential.*

Practical Magick is concerned with the Craft of Living well and in harmony with Nature, and with the Magick of the Earth, in the things of the Earth, in the seasons and cycles and in the things we make with hand and Mind.

Forthcoming books:

Temples, Groves, and Sanctuaries

In Her Image

Llewellyn's Practical Magick Series

WHEEL OF THE YEAR

Living the Magical Life

Written by Pauline Campanelli

Illustrated by Dan Campanelli

1989
Llewellyn Publications
St. Paul, Minnesota, 55164-0383, USA

*Dedicated
to
The Old Gods*

Contents

Illustrations

Diagrams & Tables

foreword

The eternal ebb and flow of human life—the cycle of birth, death, and rebirth—is reflected in the annual cycle of the seasons. As Pagans we seek to attune ourselves with the creative forces of the universe as they are manifested in Nature, whose seasonal changes are marked by the great Sabbats. The purpose of this attunement is to promote our own evolution toward Godhood and the Gods, while maintaining or improving our worldly conditions. The method we use is to perform rituals that at once express the seasonal condition and its implication for human spiritual growth. Whether solitary Pagans like ourselves, or practicing with a group or coven, the weeks between the Solar Sabbats can seem long and spiritless, and the Lunar Esbats repetitious, unless we realize that the rhythms of Nature are ever changing on a monthly, weekly, and daily level as well as seasonally, and that these gradual transitions have a timeless magic all their own. The blossoming of certain trees, the ripening of certain fruits— each is a sacred Sabbat in itself.

My husband Dan and I, because of our deep religious convictions as Pagans, have evolved a lifestyle over the past 20 years that is intimately entwined with the seasonal cycles of Nature on a daily basis. Everyone has access to the gifts of the great Goddess, and as each of these gifts comes into season, an urge is stimulated in us to celebrate with ritual.

This book is not only about the Great Sabbats and their profound significance but also about the minor Sabbats, the magic of everyday life. Paganism is a religion of great and ancient traditions far older than any other religion can claim. And these traditions are preserved and used whenever possible, because like the amulet or the ritual tool that is charged again and again, these traditions become stronger and more powerful with every usage.

This book is filled with rituals and charms that celebrate the seasonal changes on a monthly basis. The rituals are simple and easy to perform and can readily be adapted to suit any system or innovation, because innovation based on ancient tradition is the very essence of the magical power of Pagan celebration.

December

December

The sounds of December days are muffled under a blanket of snow, whether the gray and white days of falling snow, or the sunny days of blue skies and glistening snow. In the meadows few animals are seen. Only their footprints are revealed, in meandering lines that originate somewhere unseen and go to places unknown. Grasses nod their heads of grain, inviting flocks of juncos and chickadees. Cardinals, so secretive throughout the summer nesting season, now flaunt themselves on backyard feeders, and sprays of wild roseberries add a decorative touch of red to roadside and hedgerow.

The nights of December fall dark and early, and houses twinkle with strings of colored lights. Back porches are stacked with firewood, and the crystalline air is scented with wood smoke. Inside, homes are filled with firelight and candle glow, and ovens yield old family recipes, while outside, the drifting snow fills the valleys and covers the rooftops.

As others prepare for their holiday season, Pagans too begin to gather the magical and sacred greens and to carry on ancient traditions from which others have borrowed.

Baking cookies and making confections is probably a universal holiday tradition. Almost every family and every nation has its special holiday recipes. Few people today recognize the magical importance or significance of these holiday sweets; but to our Pagan ancestors, to eat these specially baked and sweetened treats at this time—when the old year was ending and a new one was about to begin—was to partake of the body of the Grain God/Goddess while insuring "sweetness" in the year to come. (In some traditions, eating something "sour" at the new year insured "sweetness" the rest of the year.) The ancient world did not have sugar but used honey as a sweetener. One traditional Italian New Year's Eve treat that no doubt dates to Pagan times is Strufoli or Pignolata.

To make Strufoli, combine four cups of flour, a pinch of salt, one tablespoon of baking powder, five eggs, and one-half cup of vegetable oil in a large bowl. Let the dough stand for an hour or two. Then roll it into long rolls one-half inch thick. Cut the rolls into one-half inch bits and deep-fry them in vegetable shortening in a skillet until golden brown.

Place the golden brown morsels in a deep bowl. When all the dough is fried, in a saucepan bring to a simmer one pound of honey, one-eighth cup water, eight ounces walnuts, and one pound candied fruit. Pour this mixture over the fried dough and toss them together. When the mixture is cooled, chocolate chips can also be added. Strufoli is served and eaten with a spoon.

Kissing under the mistletoe is a tradition that has come down to us from the Druids, although no doubt radically changed as it passed through the Christian era. Mistletoe was sacred to the ancient Druids, who gathered it from the high branches of the sacred oaks with golden sickles. White linen cloths were spread beneath so that none of the mistletoe would touch the Earth. (Once an herb has been cut for magical purposes, if it touches the ground its powers return to the Earth.)

Mistletoe was gathered not only on Yule, the shortest day of the year, but also at Midsummer, the longest day of the year. Mistletoe gathered at Midsummer does not have berries and was probably gathered for amulets of protection, whereas mistletoe gathered at Yule bears the white berries that make it an amulet of fertility. Mistletoe is evergeen, and its rootlets are golden, symbolizing the Sun. Its white translucent berries are thought to represent the semen of the Lord of the Forest.

In Old Norse the name for mistletoe is *Mistel-teinn.* The suffix *teinn* links it to German, Irish, and Cornish words that all mean "sacred tree," and *Hlaut-teinn* in Old Norse means pieces of wood upon which sacred runes have been inscribed. One ancient runic inscription reads *mistel-vel,* which has been translated to mean the power over life and death through magic.

It is fairly easy to reconstruct in our minds the rites that must have taken place in those sacred groves on the Winter Solstice over two thousand years ago, and to realize also how great their importance must have been in order to survive to this day, if only in a most disguised way.

A sprig of mistletoe or a small pouch containing leaves and twigs of mistletoe can be hung on the headboard of your bed as an amulet, with or without berries according to your intention, or the traditional berried bunch can be hung over a doorway.

The Full Moon nearest the Winter Solstice is the Oak Moon, the Moon of the newborn year, the Divine Child. Like the Divine Child who is born to die and dies to be born anew, the ancient oak has its trunk and branches in the material world of the living, while its roots, the branches in reverse, reach deep into the underworld, symbolic land of the Spirit. As the roots probe downward into the gravelike darkness of the Earth, its branches grow ever upward toward the light, to be crowned by sacred mistletoe. At this most magical time of the year, as the light of the old dying year wanes and the Oak Moon waxes to full, cast your Circle wearing mistletoe in your hair. Let this token remind you that like the oak, we too dwell simultaneously in two worlds—the world of physical matter and the world of Spirit. As you invoke the Goddess of the Moon, ask that you become ever more aware of the other side of reality and the unseen forces and beings that are always among us.

The Winter Solstice is the time when the waxing Sun overcomes the waning Sun, and this is symbolized by the struggle between the Oak King and the Holly King in some traditions. The Holly King is the death aspect of the God, and the Oak King is the aspect of rebirth, the Divine Child.

The holly tree, resplendent at this time of year with its clusters of red berries and shiny green leaves, has long been one of the most popular evergreens for Yuletide decoration. It is celebrated in the old English carol, "Deck the Halls with Boughs of Holly"; and the lyrics of the carol, "The Holly and the Ivy," although apparently praising the virtues of the god of the new religion, hint at the tree's association with a much older god of death and resurrection in the lines, "Of all the trees that are in the wood, the Holly bears the crown."

Tinne, the Irish word for holly, is closely related to the Cornish word *glas-tin,* which means sacred tree. This may also suggest that Glastonbury, long believed to be the burial place of legendary King Arthur, may have been the site of a sacred tree or grove of sacred trees.

As any horticulturist knows, it takes a male and a female holly tree to produce berries, and then only the female bears them. It is possible that in ancient times it was recognized that only certain trees bore berries and therefore gave birth to new trees. These trees may then have been considered mother trees sacred to the Goddess long before they were sacred to the Holly King.

Today wreaths are made of all sorts of materials: boxwood, grapevine, pine cones, and during World War II, red cellophane, and they are used year-round for decoration. Traditionally, wreaths were made of holly and used only as Yuletide decoration. The circle of the wreath symbolizes the Wheel of the Year, the complete cycle, recalling that *Yule* in old Anglo-Saxon means "wheel."

Although not as popular today, the evergreen leaves of the English Ivy adorn many a Victorian Christmas card and ornament. Ivy leaves, which

Decking the Halls with Holly and other Sacred Greens

are toxic, were chewed by ancients for their hallucinogenic and possibly aphrodisiac effect. A beverage called Ivy Ale is also brewed from them for ritual use. Ivy was sacred to Osiris, Egyptian god of death and resurrection, and also to Dionysus, the Greek god of the same. In England the last harvested sheaf of grain was bound with ivy vine and called the Ivy Girl. She is perceived as being in combat with the Holly Boy—a combat, no doubt, between the half of the year presided over by the Goddess and the half presided over by the God. According to the Beth-Luis-Nion tree alphabet, the ivy month is from September 30 to October 27, the time of the year when the Lady bows to the Lord. The association of ivy with holly at Yule is symbolic of the same struggle for balance at the waning and waxing of the Sun. Nicholas Culpeper, the 17th-century herbalist, placed ivy under the rulership of Saturn, the planet that rules death.

To Pagans of most backgrounds and traditions, the Sun represents the male God, and its death and rebirth on the Winter Solstice is seen as the death of the old solar year and the birth of the new, or the birth of the Divine Child, the Sun God of the new solar year. To the Egyptians he was Horus, Divine Child of Isis and Osiris; to the Greeks and Romans he was Apollo, son of Zeus and twin brother to Artemis, the Goddess of the Moon; to Norse and Anglo-Saxons he was Balder; to the Phoenicians, Baal; and to the Celts, Bel.

And so to Pagans everywhere, the Winter Solstice, or Yule, is a solar festival, and as such is celebrated with fire. The Yule Log is an ancient tradition and its burning symbolizes the blazing forth of the new-born Sun. The Yule Log is kindled with an unburned portion of the Yule Log from the previous year, and an unburned portion of it will kindle the next Yule Fire, thus symbolizing continuity. This unburned portion of the Yule Log is kept all year as a protective amulet.

The Yule Log is selected early in the year and set aside. It is traditionally of oak. Early in the season as you begin decorating the house with great sprays of fir and sprigs of holly, you might wish to adorn the Yule Log with traditional and symbolic greens as well. The bright green needles of fir represent the birth of the new year that is about to begin. The dark needles of yew symbolize death, in this case the death of the waning year. Trailing vines of ivy represent the Goddess as the female element, as do bare branches of birch, whose wintry appearance actually promises the return of Spring. Sprigs of holly with bright red berries represent the Holly King of the dying year, while the oak log itself represents the Oak King of the new year.

Any of these greens and branches can be tied together in lovely sprays and topped off with a big red bow to adorn the Yule Log. A piece saved from last year's Yule Log, if it is big enough, can be similarly adorned.

At a point during the Yule Sabbat Ritual, the candles that were extinguished at Samhain to symbolize the darkness of Winter are replaced and lit to symbolize the return of the Sun. These new altar candles will be used at Sabbats throughout the coming year. Then, as the brand from last year's Yule Log is placed on the fire, say words such as:

As the old Yule Log is consumed, so is the Old Year.

Once the brand is burning, place the Yule Log on the fire, saying:

As the Yule Log is kindled, so is the New Year begun, as it has been down through the ages, an unending cycle of birth, death, and rebirth. Every ending is a new beginning.

Then as the log blazes, chant something like:

May the Yule Log burn
May all good enter here
May there be wheat for bread
And vats full of wine.

When the Yule Log has burned out, remember to save an unburned portion to keep somewhere in your home as a powerful amulet of protection. (Although a sacred fire should never be put out, dipping a piece of the log

The Yule Log adorned with symbolic greens—Winter Solstice

in a bucket of water is all right in this case, for safety's sake.)

The ashes of the Yule Fire are magical too, and when they are cold, a small amount can be collected in a glass bottle. For protection, dip your finger in Yule Log ash and draw a pentacle on a small piece of paper. Roll the paper into a cylinder and place it in a small red bag to wear around your neck until the danger passes. When you are safe again, burn the cylinder of paper. Keep the bottle of ash until the following Yule, and at that time sprinkle it on the hearth before the fire is kindled. When the Yule Fire has died and the unburned piece of Yule Log and a portion of the ashes have been taken for amulets, the rest of the ashes should be scattered on gardens and fields to insure fertility in the coming year.

Although many modern homes are without fireplaces, the Yule Log glows on many a Christmas card, and there is a type of Christmas decoration, a length of white birch log flattened a bit underneath so that the log can't roll. On top of this log two or three holes are drilled to hold candles, and at the base of the candles, the log is decorated with greens both real and artificial. There are many such ornaments, but I have no idea what they might be called. They probably originated about the time cast-iron stoves were replacing fireplaces in the country and steam heat was warming city apartments, and there was still a need to burn the Yule Log.

The familiar words to the old English carol "Deck the Halls" still preserve for us the Pagan meaning of the Yule Log:

> See the blazing Yule before us
> Fa la la la la la la la la
> Fast away the old year passes
> Fa la la la la la la la la
> Hail the new year lads and lasses
> Fa la la la la la la la la.

"A bayberry candle burned to the socket brings food to the larder and gold to the pocket." So goes an old poem of Germanic origin. Burning bayberry candles on Christmas or New Year's Eve is another tradition that has been with us for many years. It no doubt dates to a time before candles were artificially colored.

Bayberry wax is the whitish coating on wild bayberries. It is obtained by boiling the berries and skimming off the wax. The result is a naturally scented, slightly greenish wax. It takes thousands of berries to produce a few ounces of wax. Candles fashioned of this wax must have been very special indeed, and since green is the color of growth in Nature (which at one time meant the same thing as prosperity), these candles of rare wax took on an added significance.

Burn a pair of bayberry candles on Yule as a charm to insure growth and prosperity for the new year. To enhance the magic of the candles, anoint them with Magnetic Oil (oil in which a magnetite crystal has soaked from New Moon to Full), and inscribe the rune ᚠ into the wax.

ᚠ, the rune of money, pictographically represents the horns of charging cattle, cattle at one time being the same as a man's wealth.

There is no written account of the first Christmas tree, but its beginnings go back to pre-Christian times. In ancient Greece the fir was sacred to Artemis, the Moon Goddess who presided over childbirth. The Gaelic word for fir also applies to the palm, the birth tree of Egypt and Babylonia. To the ancient Celts, certain sacred trees were called "Bele-Trees," or "Billy-Glas," meaning evergreen or immortal trees, and they are probably associated with Bel, the Sun God reborn at the Winter Solstice.

The origin of the Christmas tree is generally ascribed to Germany, and Martin Luther, the 16th-century reformer, is often given credit for it. But the German word for Christmas tree is not *Kristenbaum,* as might be expected if that were true, but *Tannenbaum,* a word obviously related to Tinne or Glastin, the sacred trees of the ancient Celts.

The name *Tin* or *Tinne* or *Tannen* was applied to a species of evergreen oak even earlier than the holly or fir. This would suggest that the Oak King was the deciduous or dying King at one time of the year and the evergreen or immortal King at the other. Tinne, or Tannen, is also the root of such words as *tanning* (of hides) and *tannic* acid, which comes from the bark of the oak.

The similarity between the Celtic and the German names may also suggest that the worship of the Oak God dates to a time when the pre-Celtic peoples built their mounds and stone circles in Saxony and Denmark. This is further suggested by the fact that burial mounds of this period in these areas contained tanned hides and coffins hewn of the split trunks of oaks.

Robert Graves places the fir in the Tree Calendar at the first day of the year, the day of the birth of the Divine Child. The use and veneration of evergreens was frequently banned by the Roman Catholic Church, proof enough of its Pagan origins.

The earliest record of an evergreen being decorated comes from the city of Riga in Latvia in the year 1510, when a group of people belonging to a local merchants' guild carried an evergreen bedecked with artificial flowers to the market place, and in an obviously Pagan ritual, danced around it and then set fire to it. This seems to be a combination of the idea of the Christmas tree as we know it and the Yule Log.

There are, however, references to a much more ancient ritual involving an evergreen being decorated. In the ancient Phrygian myth of Cybele and Attis, the beautiful youth Attis castrated himself and died. Where drops of his blood fell, violets appeared. The Great Mother Goddess Cybele, creator of Gods and Men, who loved Attis, gathered the violets and adorned a fir tree with them. She then invoked Zeus, who granted life to Attis for six months every year, and so each Spring Attis is reborn.

The cult of Cybele and Attis spread throughout the Eastern Mediterranean, and every year an evergreen was brought into the temple and adorned with violets, its trunk wrapped in white cloth like a corpse. The following day trumpets were sounded, and on the third day a priest drew blood from his arm and made an offering of it on the altar of Cybele. As night fell, the mourners became celebrants because the God had risen, and this promised spiritual survival of death for all her worshippers.

During the 14th and 15th centuries apples were tied to evergreen trees and used in Church "miracle" plays on Christmas Eve, which was called Adam and Eve's Day by the early Church. The use of apples on an evergreen tree may be associated with the tradition of wassailing, a ritual in which a group of people carried a bowl of wassail or cider into an orchard. One tree was selected to represent all of the trees. The tips of its branches were dipped in the cider, a bit of cake soaked in cider was placed in its branches, and some of the wassail was sprinkled about its roots. Sometimes ritual dances were performed by Morris Troops, who mimicked what it was hoped the tree would do in the following year—produce abundantly. Then a wassailing song was sung: "Here's to thee old apple tree, whence thou may bud and thou may blow and thou may bare apples enow."

That the apple tree was sacred is obvious from this ritual, and it is an easy step from wassailing to tying apples or other fruit to an evergreen, which was also sacred, in order to insure an abundant harvest in the coming year. But of far greater importance to ancient Pagans than the guarantee of life-sustaining food was the continuity of spiritual life as manifested in the continuing return of the seasons. And so at this darkest time of the year it was of the greatest importance to reenact the return of the seasons of plenty in order to insure a continuation of the spiritual life.

One way to acheive this was to adorn an evergreen with symbols of Spring and of plenty, and of the Gods themselves. This process began with the selection of the tree itself. If you grow your own trees, this selection is usually done early in the year. The chosen tree will be specially treated and specially pruned throughout the year.

When the time comes to cut the tree, cut a Circle in the earth around it with your athame and consecrate it with salt and water. Then stand within the Circle facing the tree and explain to its spirit:

O sacred tree
Tree of rebirth
Symbol of the Child of Promise,
I require of you
Your uppermost branches
That they may be adorned and honored
This Winter Solstice.

Tap on the upper part of the tree trunk three times with a wand or athame to drive the spirit of the tree into the lowest branches and swiftly cut through the trunk with a saw. Then sever the astral body of the tree with the white-handled knife. Always leave several of the lower branches so that the tree is not killed. These can grow into a new tree. It is traditional to leave an offering to the tree. In this case the best offering is the promise to plant a few new seedlings of the same species in the Spring.

Before bringing the tree into the house, it should be consecrated to the Gods. Asperge its branches with salted water, pass the smoke of burning incense through them, and walk around it with a lit candle saying words like:

By Fire and Water, Air and Earth
In the name of the Mother Goddess
And the Horned God
Do I consecrate this tree of rebirth.

Then set up the tree in the heart of the house. String it with lights, and with joy and celebration adorn it with your treasured ornaments, knowing full well that you are reenacting an ancient and magical rite.

The blown-glass tree ornaments that we are familiar with today originated in Germany in the 1880s, and the little village of Lauscha is famous for its glass blowers, who turned family-operated cottage industries into an international market. But prior to the production of blown-glass ornaments, most tree decorations were of paper or wax. Tree decorating reached its height in the Victorian era, and at that time the most common ornaments were of embossed lithographed cardboard, often trimmed with loops or halos of silvered wire tinsel.

The subject of these ornaments is varied. One popular theme is angels, which of course is a product of the new religion; but there are also Victorian ladies in elegant dresses, and Victorian children with armloads of toys, neither of which seems to have anything to do with religious beliefs of any kind, possibly because the late Victorian era was a time of industrialism, and a time when Darwinism had brushed aside the beliefs of the new religion in favor of the "reality" of materialism. And then there are those Victorian ornaments that are not so easily explained. One of our favorites is a chromolithographed hen on a nest surrounded by her chicks. The cardboard is enhanced with masses of tinsel to form the nest.

Gazing at a collection of blown-glass ornaments on a tree, you will notice that they can be divided into several categories. The largest of these by far is ornaments in the shape of fruits or vegetables. Prior to the wax and the chromolithograph ornaments, trees were decorated with real edibles: nuts, apples, oranges, garlands of popcorn and cranberries, homemade candies, and cookies. We have on our own tree several blown-glass ornaments, including pears, a number of clusters of grapes, a strawberry, a carrot, a cucumber, and an ear of corn. There also are countless berries in an amazing array of color and assortment of unidentified species. These so-called berries are generally acknowledged as being among the oldest of the blown-glass ornaments. There is no written record of the first time a piece of fruit or an object representing a piece of fruit was hung on a tinne or sacred evergreen, but there can be no doubt that it was done as an act of imitative magic to insure a bountiful harvest in the new year.

Probably the next largest category of ornaments is birds. There are elegant ostriches in the most delicate blown glass, and parakeets in delicate pastel shades. A group of birds from postwar Japan are of almost identifiable species, all with spun-glass tails. Most of the bird ornaments clip onto tree branches rather than hang, so that the birds appear to be perched in a natural manner (if there can be anything natural about an ostrich perched in an evergreen). It is possible that placing a bird or an object representing a bird in an evergreen tree is a charm to hasten Spring by mimicking the reappearance of migrating flocks, but there is a stronger and more direct link to early Pagan ritual. In many countries in Europe the wren was hunted on Yule morning and killed, if not driven away, in order to let its replacement, the robin redbreast, reign. Here again we encounter the Oak and Holly Kings, because each tree in the Celtic Tree alphabet has an equivalent color, number, musical note, and bird, etc. Accordingly the wren is the equivalent of the holly, where it often is seen perched, and the robin is the symbolic bird of the oak.

The European robin is not the same species as our own harbinger of Spring, the robin redbreast, which is a thrush; but early European settlers, noting the similarities of red breast and Spring migrations, named our native bird after the robin of their homeland.

The next largest group of ornaments are those shaped like musical instruments. There are French horns, lutes, drums, cellos, and horns (some of which can actually be blown). No one can dispute the importance of music and dance to Pagan ritual, and probably for this reason it was banned from time to time by various sects of the new religion.

In our collection there are at least three harps. To followers of the new religion, playing the harp is one thing they have to look forward to in that eternity they believe follows death; but to Pagans, the harp is the very symbol of the Celtic bard, of Taliesin and Meridwyn. It represents the teachings handed down from one generation to the next without ever being committed to written record. Like the Yule Log, it represents continuity, ancient and unchanging.

Then there are an assortment of various shapes that cannot be put into any category. There are carousel horses, steam locomotives and steamships, planes and paratroopers, kittens, snowmen, pagodas, and exotic elephants from India. Among those shapes are several of special interest and significance to Pagans.

There are two ornaments in our collection that appear to have been made from the same mold. One was made to hang right-side up, the other upside down. The right-side up one is in the shape of a fir tree, the Tannenbaum, or sacred tree of Germany, where it was made. The one that hangs upside down then becomes the shape of a pine cone, the fruit of the sacred fir. There also are several crescent moons—one ornament shows a radiant golden sun on one side and a silver crescent moon on the other. There are a number of acorns in several sizes and colors, and there are no less than three ornaments in the shape of oak leaves. One has a gold owl, symbol of the Goddess Athena, flying across it, but Athena, as one of the three Fates, is one aspect of the Triple Goddess. The other two have bright red acorns. The original Celtic Glas-tin or Sacred Tree, the evergreen oak, hosted an insect that produced a red gall. This was at one time thought to be a berry, and it gave the tree its other popular name, scarlet oak.

There are two ornaments whose symbolic meanings were long a mystery. The first is a frog hanging by its tail. The other is also a frog, but this one is embossed on an ornament in the shape of a leaf or flower bud. Eventually I realized that the frog hanging by its tail is not a frog but a toad. (A basic difference between a frog and a toad is that frogs have smooth skin.) There are several 17th-century spells for protection or for destroying an enemy that begin, "Hang a toad upside down and collect its spittle," or "Hang a toad upside down in your chimney," so it is possible that this ornament is a symbolic charm for protection. The second ornament, however, is a frog, and more specifically, a tree frog. The designer of this ornament may have just been expressing a sense of humor when he or she made a tree frog into a tree ornament, but he/she may have been making a potent charm as well, because the call of the tree frog, or spring peeper, is one of the earliest signs of Spring.

One last category of ornaments is the Santa Claus. He was one of the most beloved figures of our childhood. Today he can be seen on city street corners, enthroned in department stores, or doing TV commercials. His names are many and his costumes vary, but beneath it all this jolly man with the long white beard can still be recognized as another aspect of the God in one of his most recent disguises.

Santa Claus, his most popular name, is said to be a corruption of the Dutch for Saint Nicholas. Saint Nicholas was an early bishop of Myra, Lycia, in Asia Minor. According to legend, St. Nicholas, also called St. Nick, left gifts for little children in their stockings. But this St. Nick is seldom pictured as wearing the traditional clothing of a bishop. Instead, he is usually shown as wearing a greatcoat or cape, and Old Nick is another name for Woton, the Anglo-Saxon God similar to the Celtic Holly King. St. Nick is often pictured as riding a white horse, a frequently used symbol of the White Goddess, and Odhinn's horse Sleipnir is an important element in the Woton/Odhinn mythology.

Santa is also depicted as driving a sleigh drawn by eight reindeer. The reindeer, with their many-branched antlers, are symbolic of the Horned God, and it could be argued that the eight deer represent the eight Solar Sabbats, and the sleigh, the solar chariot or the boat of the Sun God of the dying year. Another clue to his Pagan identity is that he traditionally lives in the cold Northern regions, specifically, the North Pole. Symbolically, the North is the dwelling place of spirits, the land of the dead. He is the God of the old dying year, the Holly King, Lord of the Dead.

In Russia Santa Claus wears a coat of dark fur; in France, as Pierre Noel, his coat is white; and as Father Christmas in England, it is red. In Germany he is called Weinachtsmann and his coat is sometimes patched. Our own American version of the jolly fat man in the red suit was created by Thomas Nast, a cartoonist born in 1840. In Germany, too, he is also called Kriss Kringle, supposedly a corruption of the term Christ Child, an odd name for a white-haired old man with a beard. Regardless of his name or the color of his coat, he is always an old man and always wears the long white beard symbolic of wisdom and old age.

There are many lovely old ornaments of Belsnikle, the Pennsylvania Dutch version of Santa. The name alone links him to the ancient Sun God for whom Beltane was named, and that can be traced to the Phoenician *Baal,* meaning "Lord." One ornament has a beautiful chromolithographed face with mohair hair and beard, and is enveloped in white cotton batting that has been folded, stitched, and glued to represent a greatcoat with clove buttons. The ornament contains two more clues to his Pagan identity: In his hat he wears a sprig of holly, typical of many Santas, and this identifies him at once with the crowned Holly King of the old year, and in his hand he carries a bundle of birch twigs. According to the Celtic Tree Calendar, the first month of the year is the Birch Month, and in Northern countries the blossoming of the birch signaled the beginning of the agricultural year. But most significantly, the gold-crest wren, symbolic of the Holly King, was driven out and killed on Yule morning with branches of birch. This practice was carried out, actually or symbolically, in almost every country in Europe up until recent times. This is a remnant of a magical act that drove out the dying year of the Holly King in order to welcome the Oak King of the new year.

We have another clue when we recall Santa's method of entering and leaving a house. Like the faeries who entered and left their mounds via the smoke-hole, the witch who ascended her chimney on her broomstick, or the universal shaman who flew in spirit through the smoke-hole of his tent, Santa enters and leaves a house by way of the chimney.

There are also Santas portrayed as carrying sacks of toys or fir trees. The sacks of toys are a recent addition. Earlier gifts were of fruits and nuts. The fir tree, however, is sacred to the Moon Goddess, who presides over childbirth. It is also the symbol of Attis, the ancient Phrygian God of death and resurrection. According to Robert Graves, the fir belongs to the first day of the year, the day of the rebirth of the Divine Child, the Sun God, the Oak King. One ornament that depicts this aspect of the God is a chromolithographed child enfolded in cotton batting embellished with silver filigree buttons. The child has no halo but is bedecked with nosegays of rosebuds and violets, again the symbol of Attis.

At New Year's Eve the old dying year is represented by an old man with a long white beard carrying a scythe, symbolic of death, while the new year is seen, appropriately, as a new-born child. Traditionally people gather, shedding all inhibitions to await that one mystical moment, the "witching hour," that stroke of midnight that is neither the old year nor the new. That magical "time that is not a time."

To many Pagans, Yule, the longest night of the year, marks the end of the old solar year and the beginning of the new. In the symbolism and iconography of Santa Claus, there is a similar meaning. He is at once the Holly King of the old year and the Oak King of the new, who after all, are only two aspects of the same God.

Our Yuletide traditions were brought to these shores from all parts of Europe. Whether they were carried as instinctive folk memories of a Pagan past, or disguised in the clothing of the new religion by ancient wise ones so that they would be preserved, they have arrived safely. The ornaments may have hung on other trees at other times to celebrate the birth of another child. Their colors may be faded with age, their tinsel tarnished with time, but they bring the joy of a hundred Yuletides to delight the Divine Child of the Great Goddess in all of us.

January

January

With mornings of frost-feathered trees seen through ice-etched window panes, the bitter cold of January days drives us indoors to the warmth of the fireside. By the back door sunlight flashes from the icicle that hangs above the rain barrel. Flocks of starlings gather in the hackberry tree to feed on the few remaining berries, and crows search the frozen cornfields for anything they may have overlooked in times of greater abundance.

Beneath the bird feeder, the tracks of juncos and chickadees, like cuniform writing on the snow-covered ground, are thank you notes for a handful of seeds.

In the woodland garden the black berry clusters of false Solomon's-seal nod above the snow-covered ground, and the bright red fruit of jack-in-the-pulpit reward field mice for dispersing their seeds.

Yet in this seeming lifelessness of the frozen world there are signs of new life. The buds of oak and maple are beginning to swell, and in the herb garden, under the snow, the large and waxy white flowers of white hellebore are beginning to open.

When our earliest ancestors first painted images of their religious rituals on the walls of sacred caves and understood all of Nature to be inhabited by Spirit, there can be little doubt that they first reckoned time by the waxing and waning of the Moon. The primary reason for this is that the monthly cycles of the Moon are far more visible than the slow and subtle changes in the position of the Sun, even to someone who is not especially looking for repeated cycles. One of the earliest calendars known (although its use is still a controversy that may never be settled) is a 30,000 year-old piece of bone from Europe. It is pierced with variously shaped holes in a series of sevens, suggesting the quarters of the Moon, in a loop design, which represents the lunar cycle from New Moon to Full and back to the New or Dark of the Moon. The artifact, just a few inches across, describes three such lunar cycles—three months or one season.

To each lunar month the ancients assigned a name in accordance with the nature of the activity that took place at that time. The Moon of deepest

Winter is the Wolf Moon, and its name recalls a time when our ancestors gathered close around the hearth fire as the silence of the falling snow was pierced by the howling of wolves. Driven by hunger, wolves came closer to villages than at any other time of the year, and may have occasionally killed a human being in order to survive.

The wolf in northern countries was at one time so feared that it became the image of Fenris, the creature of destruction that supposedly will devour the world at the end of time. The Christian version of the myth would leave it at that, but the myth continues. Like the wolf in the fairy tale of Little Red Ridinghood, which preserves the full idea of the myth but is used only to frighten children, the wolf is slain; and the grandmother, like the world, is brought forth once more.

Because there are 13 lunar months in a year, and because the first New Moon does not necessarily coincide with the first day of the first month, the Full Moon, midpoint of the lunar month, may not always fall in the month that is given here. And because there are 13 Full Moons in a solar year, one month will have two. The second Full Moon to occur in a month is popularly called the Blue Moon. The Blue Moon does not necessarily fall in January; we have placed it here for convenience.

The Moon following the Wolf Moon is the Storm Moon. Whether you meet with a coven on the night of the Full Moon, salute Her in a solitary ritual, or simply blow Her a kiss, bear in mind the magic of this night and the nature of the storms of January. Unlike the boisterous storms of the light half of the year, which are accompanied by the clashing of thunder and the flinging of lightning bolts, the storms of January come in silence. They blanket the world in coldness in keeping with the nature of the dark half of the Wheel of the Year. But beneath the blanket of cold and silent snow, Nature rests, as we do when in the realm of the Spirit that is called death; and like those in the world of Spirit, Nature prepares for life anew.

As the light of the new-born year slowly increases and the Wolf Moon waxes full, it is a good time to look back upon that which has just ended and learn from our experiences. Bid the past farewell and let it go in order to receive the year that has just been born. Learning to let go of that which we would cling to is one of the greatest secrets of magic.

This is a time of quiet contemplation, and of long evenings by the fire. It is a time, too, when many of us enjoy the handcrafts we are too busy for in the warmer months. Some of these crafts are of ancient origin and have sacred meanings, while others are mundane, or of recent origin. Yet these too can be given magic by an act of will.

One of the most ancient of handcrafts that is not only being practiced today but is really being revived is the spinning of yarn. Spinning is the process of twisting fibers into one continuous thread. Whether it is done on a drop spindle, or a "great" wheel, whether the fiber is cotton, flax, or fleece, spinning is a magical act. The reason for this is that as the name implies, the process involves the rapid spinning of a spindle and often a wheel as well, and this rapid spinning generates energy just as the round dance generates energy. As any spinner knows, the act of spinning can induce an altered state of consciousness, and hours of spinning can leave one feeling exhilarated. In ancient Greek mythology, the Three Fates are depicted as Clotho the Spinner, Lachesis the disposer of Lots, or sometimes the Weaver, and Atropos the Unchangeable, who cuts the thread of life at death. In Anglo-Saxon mythology, The Wyrd is a Goddess of Fate that controls humankind's destiny, particularly on the battlefield, but the names of her sisters have been lost. She is, however, one of the Three Weird Sisters of Shakespeare, and these no doubt originate from the Norse Nornir, who, like the Greek Fates, are spinners. They are also associated with darkness (night) and are unquestionably the Triple Goddess of the Moon.

Just as the spinning of yarn is a magical act, so, too, can the product be put to many magical uses. Many practitioners of magic wear a cord around their waist, which is called in Latin a *cingulum*. In some traditions also, the postulants are bound with a cord for their initiation. Sometimes the cord with which they are bound becomes the one they wear as a cingulum thereafter. The purpose of this cord, like the Circle it represents, is to contain power. These cingulums, or cords, are often knotted and are specifically four and a half feet in length, so that they can be used as a compass to draw the traditional nine-foot circle. Practitioners of ceremonial magic have several knots on their cingulums with which to measure inner and outer Circles. This cord has an ancient history and appears in some of the earliest Egyptian texts as the oval that surrounds a cartouche, or name, separating it from other hieroglyphics. The oval around the cartouche is in fact a cord tied with a knot, and its purpose is to contain the magical power of the name.

Worn around the waist, this cord represents one of the seven articles of jewelry worn by many ancient Near Eastern aspects of the Goddess: Ishtar to the Sumerians, Ashtorath to the Hebrews, and Astarte to the Greeks. In the legend of the Goddess Ishtar's descent into the underworld, she must pass seven gates or doorways, and at each one she must relinquish an article of jewelry. At the fifth gateway, she must give up her girdle. The other articles of jewelry are crown, ear ornaments, necklace, bracelets, and anklets, all of which are circles, and considering the number and the position of some, they may have served to contain the power generated by the chakras. Interestingly, in later depictions of the Goddess, She is

Spinning Yarn for Magical Cords

portrayed as wearing seven necklaces, and the Celtic and Norse Goddesses wear one necklace, or torque.

Since the purpose of the cord is to contain power, consider how much more magically effective it will be if it is of handspun material. If you are spinning any cord, yarn, or thread for magical use, chant to the rhythm of the spinning wheel or drop spindle words like:

> *Fleece and Flax*
> *Spin around*
> *As you do the Magic's bound.*

There are many charms and spells that involve the use of cords or threads, which are often short pieces that can be spun in seconds. There are charms that involve tying and untying knots in a cord to control the weather, and to help you see in a dream who is trying to harm you. And there are dozens of charms that involve tying or winding a thread around all sorts of things. The purpose is almost always to bind or contain. What it is that is bound or contained determines the color that the cord should be.

There are many sources of natural dyes in the herb garden, flower garden, field, forest, and vegetable bin. A good yellow can be gotten from grape leaves, milkweed, or carrot tops. Orange to gold can be gotten from onion skins or marigold flowers, and if an iron pot is used, the same plant material will yield a deep olive green. Soft greens can be obtained from Queen Anne's lace or coltsfoot. Native American grapes or French-American hybrids yield a purple dye, while the French varieties such as Cabernet produce a stain that is not permanent. A red of sorts can be obtained from the tuberous roots of the wildflower bloodroot, but the best reds come from madder or the insect cochineal, neither of which are native and are not commonly propagated. The only natural sources of blue are indigo and woad. Dying with indigo is a lengthy process and involves the use of unstable chemicals. Dying with woad (the plant that the ancient Britains used to dye their bodies) can be done with materials found at home, but it requires pounds of leaves to impart the palest shade of blue.

Whether you dye your own thread or not, one of the most popular and expressive forms of needlework today is embroidery. Embroidery lends itself to many things magical. Altar cloths and ritual robes are especially appropriate to embellish with magical signs or symbols. You might choose to work in fiery jewel-like colors or subtle and subdued shades, in crewel yarns or in floss. In any case, there are certain stitches that are magical by their very nature, and two of these are the *chain* stitch and the *cross* stitch. The chain stitch is a series of tiny circles, each ending where it began, and each new stitch a part of the one before it; so the chain stitch is an expression in thread of the endless chain of cycles of birth, death, and rebirth. It imparts its special magic to any design where it is included, especially if it

MAGICAL STITCHES

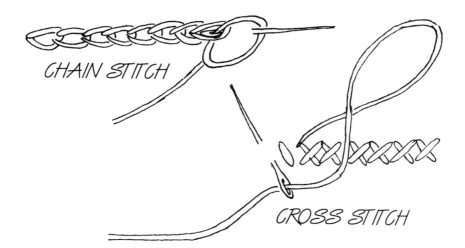

CHAIN STITCH

CROSS STITCH

SPIRALS IN
CHAIN STITCH

A SOLAR CROSS
IN CROSS STITCH

A LADDER
IN CROSS STITCH

A SUN
WHEEL

MEANDERS

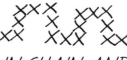

IN CHAIN AND
CROSS STITCH

forms a circle or ring, as it would if used around the hem of a garment. On the other hand, the cross stitch expresses the union of any two complements, such as male/female or light/dark.

There is a family of protection charms that involve stuffing a small jar with short pieces of colored thread. Traditionally, the pieces of thread must be put into the jar one at a time. This in itself can be an impossible task, but for the prolific embroidery artist, such a charm can be a natural byproduct of his or her work. Keep a small jar in your work basket, and each time you snip a thread from your embroidery work, put it in the jar, with words such as:

> *Thread charm*
> *Protect from harm.*

When the jar is completely full but not tightly packed, draw or paint a protective pentagram on the lid and put it on the jar. Then place it in your attic where the mass of threads will act as a tangle net to ensnare any evil that is directed at you.

Amulet bags made of cloth can be decorated with all sorts of embroidery. Large amulet bags can be made in a wide variety of colors, but a neutral black or white or unbleached muslin may be the best choice because eventually this bag might contain a number of amulets consecrated to different purposes, each in its own small cloth bag of specific color. If the amulet bag is to be embellished with embroidery, a great variety of symbols might be used, but a very powerful and practical form of decoration is encircling bands. These can be made up of magical symbols, signs of the zodiac or rune row, or abstract designs in symbolic colors. Whatever the details of the design, the encircling bands have the effect of containing the power of the amulets within the bag.

As amulets are acquired and consecrated, they can be wrapped separately or put into individually colored cloth bags or pouches so that each amulet is insulated from the others. Aside from removing amulets from the bag to draw on their magic for a specific purpose, it is a good exercise to mentally visualize or recall each one of the amulets in the bag and feel the magic it contains. This has the effect of maintaining a rapport and keeping a channel open between you and each of the amulets.

Amulet bags can be very attractive and can be worn at the waist or carried like a purse. They can also be hidden in a pocket or worn under clothing, but they should be worn or carried on the person as much as possible, and just caressing the bag can do much to recharge the psychic batteries. The only drawback to wearing an amulet bag is that it is likely to attract attention. If this happens, under no circumstances yield to the temptation to open the bag and show the contents. Not only are amulets extremely personal, but there is a very real power to secrecy. The power of the amulets will be diminished by being shown because "power shared is power lost."

The patchwork quilt was born in America, and although the craft of making them never really died out, it is now seeing a renaissance. This particular folk art does not really have a magical history or background, but it does have many elements that relate to magical thinking.

The process of making a quilt is twofold. Both parts are lengthy and require patience and attention to detail, giving the quilter ample time to impress her or his will into the fabric of the quilt. The first part of the process—the piecing—involves stitching together small pieces of colored cloth to create an overall pattern. The second part, the quilting, involves stitching together the finished patchwork, a layer of filling, and a backing. This quilt stitching will form another, more subtle, pattern over the patchwork.

Although quilt patterns were originated by Christian pioneer women of the 18th and early 19th centuries, many of the patterns will be familiar or meaningful to Pagans. Quilt patterns are of two types: a single overall design, or one made up of a small design repeated many times. Of the overall designs the majority are eight-pointed stars. Whether they are called Lone Star, Star of Bethlehem, or California Star, to Pagans they are Sun symbols, and the eight points are the eight Solar Sabbats. Some of these stars are made up of small pieces in a radiating design, while others have a square in the center divided into nine smaller squares. The number nine is sacred to the Goddess, so to a Pagan the combination might represent the Sun and the Moon or the God and the Goddess. Among the quilt designs made up of smaller squares or blocks, some squares are divided into either nine or four smaller squares, called Nine Square and Four Square respectively. There also are a group of quilt designs called Log Cabin, in which strips are stitched together to form squares. Both Four Square and Log Cabin designs are symbols of the Earth.

Whether it is a Log Cabin, a Nine Square, or a Four Square, most patterns are derived from the balanced and harmonious juxtaposition of light pieces against dark pieces. To the Pagan this idea expresses the balance and harmony of the universe as created by the Gods, which is reflected in the light and dark halves of the Wheel of the Year, the phases of the Moon, and all the rhythms of Nature.

The number of blocks that make up a quilt can also be important. A large eight-pointed star might be repeated nine times to make up the pattern of a quilt, expressing a balance between Sun and Moon, God and Goddess, male and female. A quilt might be made of a single large block containing a Sun symbol; or it might be made of 13 rows of 13 small blocks, making a total of 169 blocks, one of the numbers most sacred to the Goddess.

There are many specific magical purposes for which a quilt can be made. A quilt for healing might be made in one single eight-pointed star design representing the healing, life-giving properties of the Sun. If the color red is used, it will give vital energy to the quilt.

If a quilt is made of 13 rows of 13 blocks each, in deep indigos, it can help one who sleeps under it to have clairvoyant, prophetic, or mystical dreams.

A quilt made with a balance of Sun and Moon symbols and light and dark colors will bring harmony to the couple who sleep under it, and will probably improve their ability to work magic together as well. Early quilts that were made as bridal gifts had hearts stitched into the quilting design.

The Dresden Plate design, one of the few based on the circle, will protect the one who sleeps under it, especially if it is worked in shades of blue.

The Pine Tree design, one of the oldest quilt patterns, represents to a Pagan the Tinne or Tannenbaum, or sacred tree of birth and rebirth, and a quilt made with this design gives its blessings to new beginnings for anyone who sleeps under it.

Quilts with Four Square or Log Cabin designs have fertility magic and will aid those wishing to conceive a child, and also those who are involved with agriculture.

Making a quilt can take from a few weeks to a year or more, so it is not easy to create a ritual for making one, but you can magically charge a quilt you are about to make by following a few steps: Assemble all your materials together—fabrics, cut pieces of calico, needles and thread—and as you stitch the first two pieces of cloth together, with the very first stitch state firmly:

> With this stitch
> The charm's begun!

From then on, each time you work on the quilt or sit down at the quilting frame, hold in your hands the material you plan to work on during that session. Visualize clearly the purpose you are making the quilt for and then release the energy into the fabric. You may wish to cast a Circle around yourself each time you work, and burn incense or light a candle of the appropriate color. When you have finished the quilt and are about to tie off the very last stitch, state something like:

> With this knot
> The Magic's bound!

Whether you make a quilt yourself, commission a craftsperson to make one for you, or buy one already made for yourself or as a gift, it can

SOME MAGICAL QUILT DESIGNS

LOG CABIN

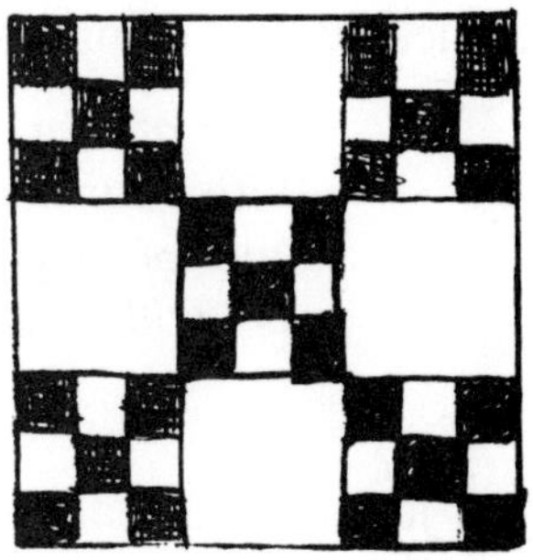

NINE SQUARE

A TREE OF LIFE

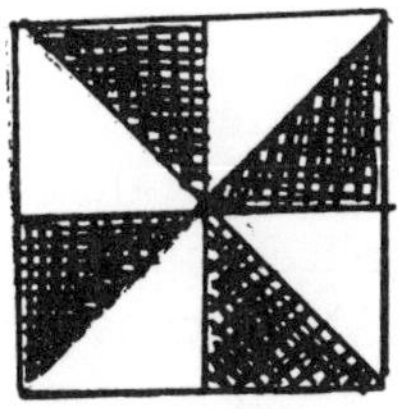

SUN WHEEL
FOUR SQUARE

ANOTHER
FOUR SQUARE

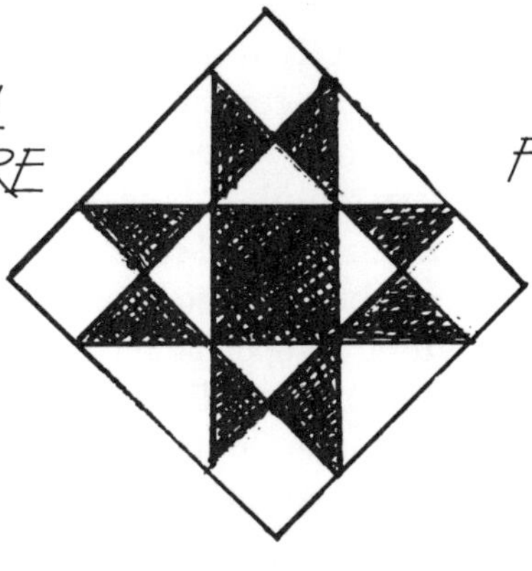

AN EIGHT-POINTED STAR

be consecrated in the four elements and in the names of the Gods and dedicated to the purpose for which you intend it, with words such as:

> *Quilt of fabric and of thread*
> *With your power protect my bed.*
> *Quilt of magic stitchery*
> *As I will, so mote it be!*

January, too, is a good time to weave baskets for use in the coming months. Basket weaving is an ancient skill and was practiced the world over. It almost always involves the use of materials that are either sacred in themselves or closely associated with the Gods. Baskets are woven of splints of oak, which is sacred to the Druids; of ash, the World Tree of the Norse; of wicker or willow, which is sacred to Hecate and is the root of the word *Wicca;* and they are also made of straw, which is derived from grain sacred to the Goddess in her aspect as the Earth Mother.

The patterns in which baskets are woven also have symbolic meanings. Baskets of splints are woven on the principle of one splint going over and under a row of vertical staves, creating a series of intersections or Solar Crosses. Like the cross stitch, these symbolize the joining of two complements, Yin and Yang, Sky Father and Earth Mother, Spirit and Matter, the union from which all life proceeds. Wicker is woven on this principle, too, and in ancient times fortifications were woven, like baskets, of flexible saplings and strong oak staves. So wickerwork brings with it the added idea of protection.

Baskets woven of straw, rye straw, or sweet grass are made on an entirely different principle: the spiral. Long bundles of straw are bound with a lashing material such as reed, and the bundles are wound in a tight coil that spirals around and around until the basket is finished at the rim. The spiral, of course, is sacred to the Goddess and symbolizes the cycle of birth, death, and rebirth. Coil baskets made by Native Americans have been made so tightly and perfectly that they can hold water.

Not only are baskets made on certain sacred principles, but the uses to which they have been put are also sacred. The ancient Egyptians left baskets of food in the funerary temples of the dead; the vanished tribes of North American Indians built their sacred ceremonial mounds with baskets full of earth; ancient Europeans buried their dead in wickerwork coffins; the harvesting of grapes, the winnowing of sacred grain, and the gathering of magical herbs were all done with baskets. From baskets of May to the harvest baskets that delineate the Lammas Circle, there has always been a close association between the celebration of the seasons and the humble craft of the basket weaver.

As the lengthening days of January draw to a close, with melancholy sunsets that are reflected on the glazed surface of the snow, we enjoy the warmth and comfort of the house. Hearts and fingers move to the rhythm of the spinning wheel and chanted word. The strange perfume of the paper-white narcissus blooming on the window sill mingles with the scent of wood smoke, hinting at the myriad of flowers that even now beneath the frozen crust of earth are beginning to stir.

February

February

The gray skies of February deliver first snow, then sleet, then rain to turn the snow and sleet to slush. But indoors there is still the warmth and good cheer of evenings by the fireside and tales told of ancient mystery and magic.

In the herb garden beneath the receding blanket of snow, some herbs begin to show the evergreen of Winter leaves. Thyme gives its flavor to a bowl of steaming soup, and salad burnet garnishes a dish of Winter squash.

In fields and meadows all plant life seems asleep, frozen in the deathlike sleep of Winter. Yet the warmth of living things, though still slumbering underground, stirs and melts the snow in ever-widening circles.

But there is sunshine, too, and the warmth of the waxing Sun has brought the hellebore into fullest bloom, while the woody branches of witch hazel burst with fragrant and exotic yellow flowers.

As dormant seeds, hidden in the cold, damp earth stir with life as yet unseen, something in us, too, begins to quicken as our spirits heed the promise of the rebirth of Nature.

Now is the time for the banishing of Winter. On the first night of February, the eve of Imbolc, gather together all of the greens that adorned the house throughout the Yuletide season, including a branch or two of the fir tree that was hung with holiday ornaments. Then, as a part of the Imbolc Sabbat rite, add these greens to the Sabbat Fire (a little at a time, and carefully, because by now they are hazardously dry), dancing and chanting all the while with words like:

> *Now we banish Winter!*
> *Now we welcome Spring!*

Another wonderful ritual that has become a part of the Imbolc Sabbat is the ritual known as Bride's Bed. Last year at the time of the Autumnal Equinox, a bundle of grain or a bunch of corn was ritually brought into the

Sweeping the Magic Circle

house. In ancient times this would have been the last sheaf of wheat or the last row of corn harvested. It was believed that the Spirit of the Grain or the Goddess Herself resided in the last grain harvested (where it had retreated). This last of the grain of the old harvest is then the seed of the next harvest. It is another link in the endless chain of immortality, the continuous cycle of birth, death and rebirth.

Some of the names given to the bundle of grain are the Corn Mother (or Barley, Oats, or Rye Mother), the Harvest Mother, and the Sheaf Mother. This bundle, if it is of grain, is often made into the shape of a human figure and dressed as a woman in white clothing. It is then the Corn Bride or Corn Maiden. If it is a bunch of corn, then the ears might be of three different colors representing the three aspects of the Goddess.

If the Corn Bride has not already been "dressed," then she can be dressed as a part of the Imbolc rites. The bridal dress can be as simple or as realistically detailed as you wish. When she is dressed, place her in a basket or on a square of white linen, with the Priapic Wand (an acorn-tipped wand of oak described in the next chapter) entwined with ribbon. Place the Wand across the Corn Bride so that they form an X, then place a pair of new candles that were lit as a part of this Festival of Lights on either side of the bridal couple and chant something like:

Blessed be the Corn Bride!
Blessed be the Great Mother!

After chanting this three times, extinguish the candles.

At sunrise the following morning (February 2), as the ground hog searches for his shadow, place the Corn Bride (minus her wedding dress) on the front door of your house, where just the night before perhaps a wreath of holly hung. This Corn Bride is an amulet of prosperity, fertility, and protection. It will also be a sign that yours is a Pagan home where the ancient Gods are welcomed and venerated. The corn can remain until after Halloween, but should be returned to the natural cycle before Yule. It can be scattered in fields or used to feed birds during the harshest Winter weather.

The Moon following the Storm Moon is the Chaste Moon. Like Diana, chaste Goddess of the Moon, all of Nature at this moment is pure potential waiting to be fulfilled. The Goddess has many forms: the Maiden pure and lovely as the snow of February, the seductive enchantress of the night, or the Crone ancient and wise. As the Goddess can change Her form according to the Moon or according to Her will, ever renewing Herself, ever beginning again, so can we, Her children, always begin again by discovering new potential within ourselves. When you have cast the Circle of the Chaste Moon, when the candles have been lit and the incense burned, look

Bride's Bed — Imbolc

deep within yourself to discover what potential lies there waiting, like the Maiden, to be fulfilled.

Through the weeks ahead the days grow gradually longer, but this is still the dark half of the year presided over by the Spirit Father and the Goddess in Her dark aspect of the Crone, teacher of things hidden and secret. This is the time to develop those nonphysical skills so necessary to the working of magic. These include prophecy, clairvoyance (including clairaudience, clairsentience, etc.), psychometry, telepathy, and psychokinesis. The common thread that connects all of these is the opening up of psychic channels that enable us to perceive the flow of subtle information we are constantly receiving but are seldom aware of.

The first of these skills, *prophecy,* is the art of foretelling the future. For the Wiccan there are numerous ways of accomplishing this. Many of these methods involve the use of artificial devices such as Tarot cards or runes. Even a simple pendulum can answer questions pertaining to the future if it is held over some form of the alphabet like that on a ouija board.

Though it is not necessary to perform these rituals of prophecy within a Circle, it is important to create an atmosphere hospitable to them. It might be helpful, for instance, to purify the area you will be doing your reading in by performing a simple banishing ritual. Walk around the area with a censer, burning a small amount of wormwood, and intone words such as:

> *By the power of this smoke*
> *I order ye, unfriendly*
> *And negative influences,*
> *Be gone!*

(Asperging the area with fresh sprigs of rosemary, wormwood, and vervain dipped in spring water is also effective.) Light a white candle and burn some sandalwood incense, sit quietly and achieve a meditative state, and then begin the reading.

Methods of divination that involve the use of devices such as Tarot cards or runes require not only the cultivation of subtle abilities but also the learning of complex systems of symbols as well, both divinatory and esoteric. These symbols, chosen at random, act as both a focal point and a catalyst to stimulate the subtler levels of our perceptions.

Scrying, or crystal or mirror gazing, is another method of using an external object as a focal point, but it does not require learning a system of symbols. The origin of both crystal and mirror gazing is probably the traditional "Black Mirror." This is a small earthenware bowl, small enough to be held in both palms. To make it into a scrying mirror, hold it inverted over a candle flame until the interior is entirely covered with black soot. Then gently fill the bowl with pure water, without disturbing the soot.

If you don't want to make a Black Mirror, an ordinary mirror or a crystal ball will work just as well. Crystal balls and mirrors show the future by acting as focal points in which the mind's eye can perceive images. These images must then be interpreted. The mirror, along with the comb, are symbols of the Goddess. The power of the mirror as well as the crystal ball will be increased by washing it monthly with an infusion of mugwort and then leaving it overnight in Moonlight, where it can be charged with the magic of the Moon.

Prophetic dreaming, or "dreaming true," is a spontaneous method of prophecy that involves no external devices. Everyone dreams every night, and sometimes these dreams are prophetic or clairvoyant. The difficult part is remembering and interpreting them. A few things can help: Before going to bed, place a notebook that is to be used strictly for recording your dreams next to your bed. Under your pillow place a small cloth bag of a mystical color—violet, indigo, or black. This bag should contain a pinch of mugwort and a length of red string with the two ends tied together in a knot so that the string forms a circle. Then lie down and chant words like:

Charm of Mugwort,
Charm of String,
Dreaming True,
And Remembering.

Chant this three times before drifting off to sleep. This should not be done every night, because it can interfere with the pattern of normal dreaming vital to mental and physical health, but it should be done frequently enough so that a channel is kept open for prophetic and clairvoyant dreams.

Clairvoyance, or "far seeing," and the related *clairaudience* and *clairsentience* ("far hearing" and "far feeling"), can be practiced with the help of a friend. The friend should be someone whom you can psychically spy on and who can later verify your impressions.

The psychic phenomenon known as *astral projection* may very possibly be clairvoyance in the extreme, or more likely, a combination of clairvoyance, clairaudience and clairsentience—an experience so vivid that it was just like being there. In recent experiments performed to verify (or disprove) clairvoyance, many of the subjects described the target areas as if they were seeing them from above. This is a perspective more commonly associated with astral projection than with clairvoyance. Both clairvoyance and astral projection, then, seem to be a matter of consciousness leaving the body to go to a distant place and bring back information in the form of an experience. The degree of consciousness that leaves the body determines whether the experience will be considered clairvoyance or astral projection.

This experience should be of interest to Wiccans because astral projection is usually considered to be the explanation given for the legendary flights of Witches on broomsticks. The ability to astral project may also have been enhanced by the application of hallucinogenic flying ointments. The famed psychic Eileen Garret described her consciousness as a hawk flying out from her, grasping the necessary information in its talons and returning.

If you have a besom, or Witches' broom (which will be discussed in greater detail in the next chapter), there is an exercise that you can do repeatedly to develop the skills of clairvoyance and astral projection. Sitting quietly in a dimly lit room, anoint your forehead with Altar Oil or Air fluid condenser (oil- or alcohol-based liquid in which herbs, metals, or gems with Air qualities have been steeped), making the sign of the pentacle. Burn an incense that contains patchouly. Have your broom or besom within reach. Breathe deeply and rhythmically for as long as it takes to achieve a deeply meditative state. Then slowly, in your imagination, rise from your chair and take the besom in your hand. Straddle the besom and slowly walk in a circle sunwise several times. Feel yourself becoming lighter and lighter, your feet no longer touching the floor. Your weight, what little there is, is totally supported by the broomstick. Now point its handle toward the open window where the moonlight is pouring in. You will fit through the open window easily—size is not a factor. Once outdoors, gain a little altitude. If it is a wintry night you will not feel cold. Circle over the place where you live and get your bearings. Then point your broomstick in the direction you wish to go. If it is on the Earth Plane, take note of any unusual sights below. When you have arrived at your destination, observed your surroundings, and obtained whatever information you required, point the broomstick in the direction of home. The return trip can be fast, so slow it down by retracing your steps and observing details. When you are back indoors, gently let your feet touch the floor. Return the besom to its original position and then lower yourself back down into your physical body.

If the place you visited was on the Earth Plane, it may be possible to verify any details later on. This kind of positive feedback is vital to psychic development and helps to separate truly psychic information from simple imagination or mental static. Imagination is extremely important to magical workings, but if it is accepted as information gained psychicly, it can lead to self-deception. Great psychics in ancient times were deeply respected because their abilities were the result of strict discipline.

Telepathy is mind-to-mind thought transference. It usually refers to the transference of thought between the minds of living individuals, but *mediumship* is the communication between the mind of the living individual and that of one who has crossed over into the lovely realm of Spirit. Depending upon the development of the discarnate entity, the mediumship might be called artistic or poetic, spiritual, or even divinely inspired. It should be remembered that highly evolved entities would never consider intruding into the mind of another individual. Telepathy, on any level, must be voluntary. Even telepathic messages received in the dream state can only be received when the dreamer intentionally places him/herself in this receptive state.

In order to become a successful telepathic receiver, it is necessary to learn to meditate. This is necessary for two reasons. The first is that the process of learning to meditate teaches you to understand the chain of connected thoughts that are a part of normal mental activity, so that you can distinguish a prophetic vision or a telepathic communication from the normal stream of consciousness. The second reason is that meditation eventually controls the mental static so that you can make yourself receptive to telepathic messages at will.

In order to practice telepathy you may want to work with a friend, taking turns "sending" and "receiving." At the appointed time, light a pale blue candle, anoint your forehead with an Air fluid condenser or oil, and burn an incense of patchouly. If you are to send, breathe rhythmically, and when you feel that you are centered, develop a clear image of the message. Hold it for a minute or two, seeing it as clearly as possible and in enough detail to make it realistic. Then with an exhalation of breath, release the image as you visualize your working partner receiving it. If you are to receive the message, follow the same procedure as above; but once your mind is quiet, visualize your partner. Concentrate on this image for a minute or so and then ask it, "What is the message?" Listen quietly for the answer.

Exercises such as these can attune your mind to receiving messages that may be important to you. As a practical daily activity—while brushing your hair, or washing dishes, or doing any chore that does not require attention—visualize what you will be doing later in the day. Create an image of the place you will be at. (If you don't know yet what it looks like because you've never been there, try to create the picture anyway, then later see if you were right.) Visualize the place as clearly as possible and then let the scene unfold. Notice if anything unusual happens. Then visualize the key people in your life wherever they may be. One at a time, see them as clearly as possible and ask whatever question seems pertinent: "How are you?," "What are you doing?," "What's new?," and without letting wishful thinking or worry interfere, listen quietly for an answer. Then send each one a blessing in turn. This exercise keeps a psychic channel open between you and your loved ones, and it is an excellent way to practice prophecy on a daily and practical basis.

If it is communication with discarnate entities that you are interested in, there are several devices that can be used. One of the simplest of these, the wineglass, is fully described in the October chapter. It is not unlike the infamous ouija board. In both cases, an object is slid around on a board that has an alphabet on it. The object, planchette, or wineglass spells out messages by moving from one letter to another. A pendulum can be used in the same way if held over an alphabet. None of these objects are dangerous in themselves, but they have been the objects of so much fear and ignorance that they do have about them an aura of negativity, especially the ouija board. So if you plan to use one of them, it is best to perform a banishing ritual such as the one mentioned earlier in this chapter. Then light a candle of indigo or violet, which will attract higher entities. The power of the candle will be enhanced if it is dressed with Altar Oil (described in the November chapter), and inscribed with the ⌠ rune. Then burn frankincense and place your fingers on the wineglass or planchette (or hold up the pendulum) and ask the traditional, "Is anyone here?"

If you plan to make a wineglass, ouija board, or pendulum a part of your regular practice, it should be cleansed and consecrated within a Circle before an altar. First purge it in the smoke of wormwood (even if it is brand-new), saying:

> I purge ye by this smoke
> That all evil influence be cast out.
> As I will, so mote it be!

Then anoint it with Altar Oil, saying:

> I anoint thee that thou be
> A vessel of good intent.

Then consecrate it with salt and water, incense and candle flame, saying:

> By the power of the Elements
> In the name of the God and Goddess,
> I consecrate this board
> That it may aid me
> In my magical work.

If telepathy is mind-to-mind communication, then *psychometry* is object-to-mind communication, and this is one of the most important psychic skills to the practitioner of magic. There has been a theory put forward to explain both haunted houses and psychometry. This theory states that on an almost physical level, objects that are present during an emotional crisis, a physical tragedy, or an act of violence are somehow emotionally charged, like a magnetic tape, and that anyone who later comes into contact with the object may be able to see or experience the event. But this theory doesn't hold up on two counts. First, if this theory were true, places such as Civil War battlefields, where thousands of men died in agony, would be unapproachable by anyone with the least bit of sensitivity; and second, the majority of hauntings are not reenactments of dramatic tragedies but of mundane chores, such as washing dishes or sweeping. Psychometry, on the other hand, is the use of an object to form a telepathic link with the mind of another human being. This is one of the most basic elements of magic: A bit of hair, fingernails, a photo, clothing, or a possession of another person can all be used to perform magic for the harm or for the good of that individual, because these objects form a psychic link. Inanimate objects can also be used by the practitioner to receive magic, because psychometry is a two-way street.

This is a skill worth developing. It can be practiced with the help of a friend who is willing to bring you an assortment of objects with known histories for you to "read." Your working partner can also help you with the opposite side of psychometry—the charging of objects. Select several pebbles of similar appearance from the same environment. Number each one, and on a piece of paper write the numbers. Next to each one write a feeling: love, safety, etc. Then within a Circle and before an altar, select one of the pebbles and light a candle of the appropriate color. Holding your wand straight out in front of you, visualize in symbol form the feeling you plan to charge the pebble with. Then as you inhale, visualize the power of this feeling being drawn into the wand through the tip. Feel it intensify for a moment, and then point the wand at the pebble. As you exhale, see the energy flow from the wand into the pebble.

To test your abilities, have your working partner psychometrize the pebble (assuming he or she has a fairly well-developed ability to do so). This kind of testing and positive feedback of results was the basis of magical apprenticeships of ages past. This or similar methods can be used to psychically charge amulets and charms that may or may not already have their own natural powers. Some of the most powerful magic was performed in this way. The little Egyptian figures called Ushabti were psychically charged through a lengthy ritual that took several days, so that they could take the place of the deceased in the next life when it was time to do agricultural chores. Thought forms that guarded and still guard the tombs and treasures were produced by priests who psychically charged their protective inscriptions.

The last and most difficult to acquire psychic skill is *psychokinesis*—the ability to move objects with the mind alone. The greatest barrier to achieving this is the mind itself, and the doubts therein. What makes all the other skills seem more possible is that they can all be explained as coincidence. But magic is the ability to cause change in accordance with one's will, so this skill is well worth developing.

To practice psychokinesis, you could buy some really expensive equipment designed to record the slightest change in the Earth's electromagnetic field, or you could tape a pendulum of some kind on a fine thread onto the inside of a mayonnaise jar lid so that when the lid is tightened on the jar the pendulum is suspended within. If you make such a device, place the jar on a steady surface and seat yourself before it. Gaze at the pendulum within the jar, willing it to move. Visualize it beginning slowly to swing around. Most likely after a while a picture will fall off a nearby wall, or the window shade directly across the room from you will fly up, sounding like a gunshot. But these of course are just coincidences. The pendulum in the jar just hangs there while you are getting a headache from mentally screaming, "Move, dammit!" Now gently reach out and shake the jar, because it doesn't really matter how you cause change to occur in accordance with your will as long as it occurs. With natural magic the results always seem to happen in natural ways, no matter what the odds.

At mid-month is Valentine's Day, named for a third-century priest of the new religion who, according to legend, was condemned to death by Claudius II, emperor of Rome. While St. Valentine was in prison, he noticed violets growing outside his cell window. He picked some of the heart-shaped leaves and pierced the words "remember me" or "remember your Valentine" into the leaves and then sent them, via a friendly dove, to his friends and loved ones. (Another legend has it that he cured the blind daughter of his jailkeeper.) St. Valentine has since become the patron saint of love.

For centuries before the reign of Claudius II, the 15th of February was the date of the Roman celebration of Lupercalia, during which the priests of Faunus, an ancient god of fertility, went about the streets of Rome dressed in goatskin loincloths, carrying thongs with which they struck women across the palms in an ancient fertility rite. The day prior to this, the 14th of February, was sacred to the Goddess Juno, Queen of the Heavens and personification of the three aspects of the Goddess. On that day young men drew lots to choose their female partners for the festivities. Centuries later, a similar custom was still practiced in England and Scotland.

The little figure of the winged child with bow and arrows that appears on so many Valentine cards—whether lovely, lacy Victorian ones or contemporary Valentines—is Cupid, the son of Venus, Roman Goddess of Love. Cupid fell in love with Psyche, a girl so beautiful that Venus became jealous of her and through trickery and deceit caused Psyche to descend into the underworld of Hades, Land of the Dead. Cupid, however, discovered her and brought her back to life, and through his love Psyche became immortal.

Valentine's Day, with its roots in the ancient fertility rites of the Lupercalia, in the worship of Juno, and in the love of Cupid for Psyche, is a celebration of the heart. To practitioners of yoga and other Eastern traditions, the heart is the seat of the fourth chakra. Like the number four in some systems of numerology, it is a pivotal point between two triads. The heart chakra is the connecting link between the lower triad of the chakras of physical manifestation and the upper triad of the chakras of psychic and spiritual existence. The chakras open in sequence: The upper triad of chakras cannot begin to open until the heart chakra opens. So celebrate this day of the heart, this midway point of February. Take this opportunity to express your love and open your heart chakra a little more.

Light pink candles and burn sweet incense. Sit quietly and visualize yourself surrounded by a luminous pink cloud. Inhale the rose-scented pinkness of the light and feel it filling your heart with love, and share the love with someone.

As the February Sun waxes and the Storm Moon wanes, the days grow slowly longer. Catkins hang on birch and hazel trees, and maple buds seem ready to burst. Like ourselves, all of Nature awaits the coming of Spring.

March

March

The delicate birch twigs that etch the clear blue skies of March now dangle with catkins, and the gray, fuzzy buds of the pussy willow swell. Brave crocus break through the still-frosty ground, opening their petals to the Sun. Beneath the blanket of leaves that has covered the herb garden throughout its long Winter's sleep, the peppermint is sending out new runners, and tiny whorls of woodruff leaves dot the ground. In the woodland garden, patches of moss grow a thick, lush green, and the strange and exotic flowers of the skunk cabbage bloom.

A love-struck starling throws back his head and sings a courting song to his mate, who already wears the sleek, black feathers of Spring, while in the open meadows flocks of migrating robins graze in the still-brown grass. In the hedgerows, cock pheasants, like phoenixes come to life from an ancient Chinese vase, challenge one another with fierce displays of feathers and spurs.

The pruning season begins about mid-month, and even though the Vernal Equinox has not yet been celebrated, this is the time to begin gathering wood for the Beltane Fire. A good Beltane Fire should be made of nine different kinds of wood. A bundle of three pieces of each kind is ideal. A good combination of woods are

Birch, representing the Goddess or female principle. In Northern European countries, the goddess of Spring, or the Maiden, is seen as the Birch Goddess. The budding of the birch signals the beginning of the agricultural year. In Celtic countries the robin redbreast of Spring carries in its bill a sprig of birch with which to drive out the gold-crest wren of the old year. Everywhere the birch is a symbol of fertility, so add birch to your Beltane Fire to represent the Goddess.

Oak, symbolizing the God or male principle. In Celtic countries the Druids worshipped in sacred oak groves, and used every part of the oak for ritual purposes. In fact, the name "Druid" comes from *Duir* (oak) and *wyd* (wood). It is also from the oak that the Druids gathered the sacred mistletoe, the white berries of which were seen as representing the semen of the Lord of the Forest, linking it once again to the male principle. So add oak to the Beltane Fire to symbolize the God.

Rowan, or *mountain ash,* as the Tree of Life. It is a tree of powerful magic, and it used to be planted by cottage doors to protect against evil. According to one Celtic legend, a certain rowan tree bore fruit each quarter (that is, at each Great Sabbat), and a taste of its fruit would ward off hunger. So add rowan to the Beltane Fire for life.

Willow, as the tree of death. It is sacred to Hecate, and its association with both the dark half of the Wheel of the Year and the dark phase of the Moon link it to Witchcraft. The words *Witch* and *Wicca* have the same root as the word *wicker.* Winnowing baskets were woven of willow or wicker, and the infamous engraving of the "Wicker Man" that gave the Druids the reputation of being such bloodthirsty practitioners of human sacrifice was actually done in 1676, more than 1,600 years after the fact, by a follower of Christianity, based on one vague reference by Julius Caesar. Add willow to the Beltane Fire as a celebration of death.

Hawthorn, the tree of purification. The hawthorn, or May tree, has white blossoms and fruits that resemble rose hips. It ruled the month during which the Romans purified their temples. In some Celtic traditions, hawthorn branches were strewn in fields to insure fertility. The hawthorn is sacred to faeries and is a traditional wood for the Beltane Fire. Add hawthorn to the Beltane Fire for purity.

Hazel is the tree of wisdom. Its nuts are symbolic of wisdom, and its branches have long been used for divining rods to find the location of hidden minerals or water. Add hazel to the Beltane Fire to gain wisdom.

Apple, the tree of love. Apple wood and apple blossoms have long been associated with love. In Judeo-Christian mythology, Eve seduced Adam with an apple. Wild apple, or crab apple, was the wood that flails were made of. Flails were used to thresh grain, and they are of such ancient design that they were one of the symbols of the pharaohs of Egypt. The design never altered until the mid-1800s. Threshing was such a sacred ritual that when the Hebrew king David entered Judea, the first thing he did was purchase a threshing floor upon which to build a temple. It was also upon a threshing floor that the Celtic Goddess Cerridwen, in the form of a black hen, found Gwion in the form of a grain of wheat and devoured him. Later in her human form she gave birth to him as the wizard Taliesin. Add apple wood to the Beltane Fire for the magic of love.

Vine (grapevine), the tree of joy. The vine is not native to Britain but is included in the Celtic Tree Alphabet. It is also not a tree in the true sense, but it will grow a thick, woody, treelike trunk with age and proper pruning. Because the fermented juice of its fruit can induce an altered state of consciousness, it is sacred to Dionysus, the God of death and resurrection. Add vine to the Beltane Fire for joy.

Fir, the tree of immortality. Sacred to the Goddess of birth and rebirth, the evergreen fir tree is a symbol of the forces of life overcoming the forces of death and decay. The fir might seem out of place in a Beltane Fire, but this tree is also sacred to Attis, the God who is reborn each Spring. It is also the traditional Maypole. Add fir to the Beltane Fire for rebirth.

When the three pieces of each of the nine woods have been gathered, they can be tied in a bundle and left to dry until May Eve.

While trees are dormant it also is a good time to collect wood for wands for various purposes. The function of a wand is to attract certain types of energies, which can be directed according to your will. For this reason you may want to have wands of several kinds of wood, because different woods have different affinities. When gathering wood for magical purposes there are several steps that should be followed.

First, select a branch that should be pruned, not one that will harm the tree by its removal. This will require a bit of knowledge of the growing habits of the species.

When the branch has been selected, cut a circle around the tree with the athame. Stand within the Circle facing the tree and invoke its spirit.

> *O Spirit of the Oak I invoke thee*
> *By root and trunk I summon thee*
> *By branch and leaf I call upon thee*
> *Hear me and grant my request*
> *O Spirit of the tree.*

(It takes longer to invoke the spirit of a dormant tree than one in leaf.) Then tie a length of red cord loosely around the selected branch and ask:

> *Grant that I may take from thee*
> *This branch and that it will bring to me*
> *The power of your magic wood.*

Wait for an affirmation, such as a breeze in the branches or the fall of an acorn. Then tighten the red thread like a tourniquet and say words like:

> *Thank you Spirit of this tree*
> *Blessed be, blessed be.*

Many herbalists recommend gathering all magical herbs with the white-handled knife, but when collecting wood this isn't always possible. The easiest and most humane way to get around this is to make a clean cut

Gathering Wood for a Magic Wand

above the cord with a pruning shears or a saw if necessary, and hold the branch in its original position until its spirit is severed by cutting through the same cut with the white-handled knife.

It is traditional then to give the tree something in return. Sometimes a lock of hair is given. The American Indians gave a pinch of tobacco. A Job's plant food stick or a scoop of fertilizer will be just as appreciated.

Don't forget to remove the cord and clear the Circle, and if the cut you made was more than an inch in diameter, tar the wound to prevent bacterial infection to the tree.

The wand used for several different purposes in Spring rites, the Priapic Wand, is actually a phallic symbol. It is traditionally tipped with an acorn and is of oak.

Apple wood is good for a wand that is to be used for love, seduction, or attraction magic.

Hazel wood is ideal for an all-purpose magic wand. It was the wand of the Druids. It can be tipped with a quartz crystal and inscribed with runes or magical symbols, if you wish, before being consecrated.

Rowan, or mountain ash, one of the most magical trees in European mythology, is also an excellent wood for an all-purpose magic wand. Like the hazelwood wand, it can be tipped with a crystal, inscribed with symbols or runes, or carved.

Certain woods are also ruled by certain planets. Laurel is ruled by the Sun, willow by the Moon, hazel by Mercury, myrtle by Venus, cedar by Mars, pine by Jupiter, and oak by Saturn. A wand of the appropriate wood should be used when working planetary magic, and it can be tipped with the correct stone and inscribed in the color ink ruled by that planet.

Once you have cut the branch of wood needed for a wand, bring it into your working area and cast your magic Circle. It may need to be cut again to the proper length. The traditional length for a wand, which is a very personal tool, is equal to the length of your own arm from the elbow to the tip of the little finger. Inscribe it with the magical signs and runes and add a crystal if you like, and when it is finished, consecrate it in the elements of Earth, Air, Fire, and Water by passing it through the candle flame (Fire), and incense smoke (Air), and touching it to the pentacle of Earth and the cup of Water with words such as:

> *In the name of the Goddess and the God*
> *I consecrate this wand in the element of Earth,*
> *In the element of Air, in the element of Fire*
> *And in the element of Water*
> *That it will aid me in my magical work.*

Then holding the wand high in both hands:

MAGICAL WOODS

TREE	PURPOSE	SYMBOLIC BIRD
BIRCH	NEW BEGINNING BESOM	ROBIN
MOUNTAIN ASH (ROWAN)	MAGIC PROTECTION	DUCK
ASH	RUNE STAVES BESOM	SNIPE
ALDER	WATER MAGIC STRENGTH	GULL
WILLOW	DEATH BESOM	OSPREY
HAWTHORN	WISHING FAERIES PROTECTION	CROW
OAK	POWER MAGIC	WREN
HOLLY	MAGIC	STARLING
HAZEL	WISDOM	CRANE
APPLE	LOVE	HEN
VINE	HAPPINESS	TITMOUSE
IVY	LOVE/FERTILITY	SWAN
ELDER	NEGATIVE MAGIC	GRACKLE
FIR/PINE	BIRTH/REBIRTH	KILLDEER
POPLAR	SUCCESS	SWAN
YEW	DEATH	EAGLE

O wand of wood be now bound
To work my will at my command
Thus do I consecrate this Magic Wand.

While the trees are still dormant, there are still other materials to be collected, amulets that can be made, and spells that can be worked.

Grapevine gathered at this time of the year will remain flexible for several months. It can be made into decorative wreaths, woven into baskets, or made into symbols for ritual use, such as the Solar Disc, symbol of the Sun used both at the Summer Solstice and as a charm for bounty and prosperity throughout the year.

A traditional amulet of general good luck and protection is an *alrum*— two rowan twigs of equal length forming a solar cross and tied together in the middle with red thread. While tying the thread, chant:

Twigs of Rowan wound around
With scarlet thread the magic's bound!

The thorns of hawthorn are needle-sharp spikes from two to three inches long. They are the thorns traditionally used for piercing waxen images or for other kinds of evil magic. But they can be used protectively, too, in such age-old charms of protection as the Witches' Bottle. A Witches' Bottle has many forms, but it is basically a small bottle or jar filled with broken glass, rusty nails, old razor blades, lengths of barbed wire and/or thorns of hawthorn, then filled with your own urine and some of your own blood. With the words, "To bane to bane be gane from wence ye came!" bury the bottle upside down in a place where it will not be disturbed, as a protection against a specific act of evil magic directed against you. This charm will act as a deflective device returning the evil back to the sender.

Many such bottles have been found in England, and in 1976 on Tinicum Island in the Delaware River just south of Philadelphia, the first Witches' Bottle in the United States was discovered. Dating to the mid-1700s, it contained six pins, and beneath its shoulders were found a piece of a bird bone and a pottery shard.

The purpose of a Witches' Bottle, as was stated, is protection against a specific act of evil magic. But if you have no idea who was behind your recent run of negative situations, and you're positive it wasn't yourself, then by the law of threefold returns you will probably soon find out who it was. Observe who, within your sphere of acquaintances, has a sudden run of self-inflicted bad luck.

The thorns of hawthorn can be removed from the cut branches (they should never be removed from the living tree) with the white-handled knife and stored until needed. And if you need to make a wish, leave a strip of colored cloth tied in a hawthorn tree.

This seems as good a time as any to mention containers for all the magical materials that may be collected. It can be fun to comb flea markets and antique shops for small bottles to contain your oils and herbs, brews and potions. Old medicine bottles come in clear and pastel shades. They are available, inexpensive, and come in a variety of sizes and shapes. It is very important at this stage of the magical operation (the accumulation of basic materials) to select those objects that attract or trigger a magical response in you and to reject those that do not. As you acquire jars and bottles, wash them by hand, and when they are physically clean, purify them with a bath in an infusion of mugwort. As you fill each jar, be sure to label it. You may find that labels lettered in a Gothic-type alphabet deepen your own magical response. Remember, it is important to create an atmosphere that stimulates your own magical excitement. And while you are searching for jars and bottles, you may find just the perfect cabinet to keep all of your magical materials in.

Another tool useful in magic is the besom, or Witches' broom. Traditionally, it is made of an ash handle, a bundle of birch twigs, and bound around with willow. This besom, the broomstick of the flying crone, is primarily used for symbolically sweeping the magic Circle clean. It is also a symbol of domesticity. In some traditions a couple would step or hop over a broomstick as part of a marriage ceremony. The besom is a symbol of sexuality, and for the woman, stepping over the broomstick represented a transition from the Maid to the Mother. Standing vertically in its normal position, the broom is a phallic symbol; but inverted, it represents a woman's pubic area and the line between her thighs.

Interestingly, in Russian mythology the witch Baba Yaga rides not a broomstick but a mortar and pestle, which exhibits the same kind of dual sexual symbolism. Above all, the besom is the vehicle of the shaman, the horse upon which the shaman's spirit rides. When Odin sacrificed himself to himself, he hung crucified for nine days on his ashen spear.

Whether you make a besom in the traditional way, or purchase one that appeals to you, it is traditional to name your broom as you would a horse. Then when you have chosen a name, anoint it with oil as you would a candle, and consecrate it in the names of the Gods:

> *Besom of birch with willow tied*
> *(or besom of straw with cord tied)*
> *Be my companion and my guide.*
> *On ashen shaft by moonlight pale*
> *My spirit rides the windy gale*

> *To realms beyond both space and time*
> *To magical lands my soul will sail*
> *In the company of the Crone I'll ride*
> *This Besom of birch with willow tied*
> *So do I consecrate this magical Tree*
> *As I will, so mote it be!*

The besom is traditionally a tool used or possessed only by women, while men traditionally use a staff or a crook, which can be anointed and consecrated in a similar way.

The Vernal Equinox, that time when night and day are of equal length and the light is about to grow stronger than the dark, is celebrated about March 21. These rites of Spring should be celebrated at dawn or at dusk— that time that is not a time, no longer Winter and not yet Spring and neither night nor day. Standing within the magic Circle at this time of balance between dark and light, it is good to put Winter behind us and look forward to the light, bright months ahead and the stirrings of Nature.

Seeds that were gathered at about the time of the Autumnal Equinox, which have lain dormant throughout the dark half of the Wheel of the Year, can now be blessed in preparation for their being planted. The basket in which the separate packets were stored throughout the Winter can be kept under the altar until a point in the ritual when it will be appropriate to perform a Blessing of the Seeds. Place the basket of seeds on the altar, and using the Priapic Wand, tap each packet of seeds three times, saying:

> *Now is the dark half of the year passing*
> *Now do the days grow light, and the Earth grows warm*
> *I summon the spirit of these seeds*
> *Which have slept in darkness*
> *Awaken, stir, and swell*
> *Soon you will be planted in the Earth*
> *To grow and bring forth new fruit.*
> *Blessed be!*

As each type of seed is blessed, visualize that particular type of plant in full bloom or full fruit. Now the seeds are ready to be planted whenever the phase of the Moon is right or the days are warm enough.

As it is the time for the planting of seeds on the material plane, so may it be time to do so on the psychic planes as well. On the night that the Seed Moon of March is full, cast your magic Circle. Then before the rite has ended, select the spiritual seeds you would like to plant. They may be seeds of wisdom, seeds of understanding, or seeds of certain magical skills.

Then by an act of will, plant these seeds in the fertile soil of your subconscious mind with the firm commitment that they will be nurtured and cultivated in the months that lie ahead, so that they will grow and flower and bear fruit.

At the time of the Vernal Equinox, eggs were used for the creation of talismans and were also ritually eaten. There is little doubt that clutches of eggs laid by many different kinds of birds in the Spring were a welcome dietary supplement to early hunter/gatherers after the sparseness of Winter. It is also possible that gathering a variety of eggs from the nests of birds by our ancient ancestors gave rise to two customs still popular today—the Easter egg hunt, and coloring eggs in imitation of the various pastel colors of the eggs of wild birds. It is also believed by some that humankind first got the idea for weaving baskets from watching birds weave nests. So this may be the origin of the association between colored Easter eggs and Easter baskets.

In the Ukraine, women dye eggs in brilliant reds, yellows, and oranges. These eggs are called krashanka, and they were eaten to celebrate the rebirth of the Sun and the return of the seasons of plenty. In Italy, colored eggs are baked into braided loaves of bread for the same reason. Today there are all sorts of commercial dyes available for coloring eggs, but it is possible to dye eggs for Spring celebrations in natural dyes.

A beautiful soft orange can be achieved by boiling a single onion skin with a few eggs. A handful of onion skins will give a deep rust color.

One-half teaspoon of tumeric in a small amount of water will dye eggs a bright, sunny yellow.

Beet juice and vinegar or the juice of pickled beets will dye eggshells pink.

Boiling eggs with vinegar and several of the outer leaves of red cabbage, and allowing the whole mixture to cool overnight, produces the most amazing robin's egg blue; but be careful, because this dye scratches off easily.

During the Spring Ritual at the Vernal Equinox, bowls and baskets of naturally dyed eggs and magically inscribed *pysanky* may be placed around the circle and the colored eggs may be eaten as part of the ritual. Pysanky, the famous Ukrainian Easter eggs, are powerful amulets for fertility, prosperity, and protection, and the creation of them is an ancient ritual that evolved with the hunter/gatherers of Eastern Europe. At one time practiced only by women, this tradition has come down to us from the Pagan past with its symbolism mostly intact.

There is an ancient legend in the Ukraine that tells of a demon monster that would devour the world. This monster is chained, and as it strains

A Cabinet of Magical Herbs & Oils

Pysanky—Eggs that are Magical Amulets—Vernal Equinox

and pulls, the links of its chains are weakened. But every Spring the chain is strengthened in proportion to the number of pysanky that were made and exchanged that season.

The Ukraine did not accept Christianity as its official religion until 988 C.E., and at that time the Pagan population refused to give up this Pagan art, so eventually the Church had to accept it, give its blessing, and call them Easter eggs (which, after all, are named for a Pagan deity). And so today, along with the ancient symbols, there are Christian crosses, Orthodox crosses, church steeples, and the symbol of the new religion, the fish. Many of the old symbols have been reinterpreted to fit the concepts of the new religion. Even the legend of the chained monster has been reinterpreted to mean the struggle between good and evil rather than balance and harmony. Still, the great majority of the symbols that continue to be used today are of Pagan origin. In an egg's design, these symbols combine to create and re-create meanings in endless variety that are unique to each individual egg, because no two pysanky are ever exactly alike.

The symbolism begins with the egg itself. The golden orb of its yolk represents the Sun God, its white shell is seen as the White Goddess, and the whole is a symbol of rebirth. We know today that the egg production of domestic fowl begins when the retina of a hen's eye is stimulated by more than 12 hours of light a day. This connection between eggs and the shift of balance from darkness to light at the time of the Vernal Equinox was not lost on the Pagans of old. And so, the drawing of magical signs on a symbolic object became a charm and a ritual, to help the Sun gain strength and power over darkness at the Vernal Equinox.

The word "pysanky" comes from the root word *pysaty,* "to write," because the signs are written on the surface of the egg in a rich language of symbols almost endless in number and variation. These can be divided into three categories: animals, vegetable, and the largest by far, geometric shapes.

The most traditional way of marking an egg is with encircling bands, which represent the eternal cycle of birth, death, and rebirth. Where these bands intersect, solar crosses are formed, representing the union of Spirit and Matter or male and female, or any opposing forces. These bands themselves are composed of geometric designs each having a symbolic meaning. There are triangles representing the Three-Formed Goddess, squares representing Earth, ladders representing various planes of existence (these ladders are often made up of smaller ladders representing planes within planes), rakes representing agriculture, and pinwheels and eight-pointed stars as ancient Sun signs (the former is also a symbol of the Goddess; the latter, a symbol of the Sun God showing the eight solar festivals). Triangles and other shapes are often filled in with "netting," a series of intersecting lines that have the same symbolic meaning as the solar cross.

Rows of white isosceles triangles are "wolves' teeth," and are a powerful charm for wisdom and strength. A meandering line can mean either the rhythm and cycles of life or water, depending on the color, and the indented line, fire or water, again depending on the color. Curls and spirals give divine protection, as do the encircling bands. Dots and tiny circles are stars, which give luck and success.

Pysanky are powerful amulets that help to maintain the balance between the dark half of the Wheel of the Year, with its elements of death and decay, and the light half of growth and rebirth. But aside from their importance in seasonal ritual and magic, they are also powerful amulets for fertility, prosperity, and protection on the personal level. A woman wishing to start a family might make or be given an egg inscribed with symbols of fertility and womanhood. Her husband might receive an egg bearing the symbol of the rooster. Pysanky with powerful symbols of protection such as the encircling bands keep a home and those that dwell in it safe from psychic attack, and eggs bearing symbols of water such as a blue meander line are considered especially powerful protection against fire. In the past, if a fire did start in a house, such an egg would be carried around the fire to contain its energy and to keep it from spreading. Pysanky inscribed with wheat designs were buried in the first and last furrows of a farmer's field to insure a bountiful harvest. Most pysanky are kept in the home as protective amulets and are proudly displayed throughout the year.

The process of making a pysanky is much simpler than it sounds. It is basically a wax-resist method similar to batik. Simply put, it goes something like this: Using a tool called a *kitska* (available in some craft shops), a tiny brass funnel on the end of a plastic or wooden handle, melted beeswax is drawn onto the surface of an egg. The wax is heated in a candle flame, which turns it black so that it is clearly visible on the white eggshell. Wherever the eggshell has been waxed, it is protected and will remain white. When all of the white portions of the design have been waxed, the egg is placed in the first dye bath. Pysanky dyes are transparent, so the dye baths are always done lightest to darkest—or yellow, orange, red, then brown or black or purple. Once the egg is dyed a good yellow, it is removed from the dye bath, and any parts of the design intended to remain yellow are waxed. The egg is then placed in the orange dye bath. This process is repeated until the egg has been dyed the darkest color desired.

When the egg is removed from the final dye bath, the easiest way to remove the wax is to place the egg in a low-temperature oven, about 200 degrees with the door open a crack, until all the wax looks wet. It can then be rubbed off gently with a paper napkin, revealing the dazzling colors and stunning designs of the finished egg, which is then varnished to a high gloss.

SOME TRADITIONAL EGG DESIGNS

ENCIRCLING BANDS

INTERSECTING BANDS

A SUN SYMBOL

A TREE OF LIFE

On a day in March, while the herb garden still lies dormant under its blanket of leaves, when the crocus and snowdrops begin to push through the frosty Earth, and when the pussy-willow buds begin to break and the robins return to their ancestral nesting sites, take out the ritual tools, the kitskas, the beeswax molded in a symbolic shape, and the candle holder used only for this purpose. Carve an appropriate rune or symbol on a white candle and place it in the holder. Then select a pure white unblemished egg. (In order for it to retain its magical power, it must be raw and never blown out.) Wash the egg and warm it in your hands. Then light the candle and recite a chant asking the Goddess to accept the magic you are about to perform. Summon the power of the ancient signs and begin to draw them on the egg. The flickering of the candle flame, the incense of the burning beeswax, weave their spell as the symmetry of the egg adds its own dimension to the symbols you mark it with. After hours of concentration your gaze is fixed. Encircling bands are drawn, and the magic is bound! Extinguish the candle. An ancient ritual has been performed, a timeless tradition repeated, and the forces of Nature have been honored.

April

April

By the cellar door the ground is a mass of purple violets. In the perennial border, yellow daffodils nod above the grape hyacinth, and at the back of the garden the forsythia in full bloom is a mass of brilliant yellow, looking as if the Sun itself has come down to Earth.

In the woodland garden delicate white bloodroot blossoms push up through the downy leaves, and deep red trilliums greet the Spring. Pale hepatica rise above clusters of three-lobed leaves and the rows of white Dutchman's-breeches dangle on delicate stems in the lilac-scented air. Robins carry trailing strands of grasses back to the trees in which they've nested year after year, and lambs born in the last few months now romp and play on the greening hillsides.

Like on a lacquered Japanese screen, the white apricot blossoms burst open on leafless branches in the orchard. Everywhere new life is emerging. As bees forage in the yellow-green blossoms of the maple trees, the time has come to lift the Winter blanket of leaves from the herb garden. There the yellow dandelion-like flowers of coltsfoot, on thick scaly stems, are pushing up long before the leaves appear. The pleated leaves of lady's mantle, originally named for the Goddess, are just beginning to unfold, and the blue-green buds of cleansing rue are beginning to swell.

When all the leaves have been removed and the earth cultivated, it is a good time to do a charm to encourage growth for the season that has just begun. Walking sunwise around the herb garden, either within it or around its perimeter, asperge it with a branch of fir dipped in spring water, chanting something like:

> *Herbs that charm*
> *Herbs that heal*
> *Grow now*
> *Spring till Fall.*

All the while visualize a lush growth of foliage as your glance falls on each plant.

Now is the time to plan for any new gardens you wish to put in, and there are many different ways of arranging gardens for magical purposes. One type of garden is the sanctuary garden. This garden is dedicated to a specific deity, the God or the Goddess. If you have mature trees on your land, such a garden could be planned around either a single tree or a grove. A sanctuary garden for the Goddess, for instance, could be planted under a willow or in a grove of birch. If the conditions are right, it can be planted with plants sacred to the Goddess, such as lady's-slipper orchids, artemisia, ivy, maidenhair ferns, or Moon vines. At the center of the sanctuary, arrange three stones representing the three aspects of the Goddess to act as a vessel for Her spirit if She should wish to reside there at any time, or a single large stone with a natural hole in it. This is a perfect place for receiving or pouring libations and for making offerings of flowers or other tokens of love. It can also be a place to put the offerings made indoors at the Sabbats.

A sanctuary garden for the God would be appropriate under an oak or in a grove of oaks, or in a grove of oak and holly. In the center of the grove, one tall, narrow standing stone, or *menhir,* is an excellent vessel for the God. If the right standing stone cannot be found, a column of stones can be constructed by piling one on top of the other.

Another arrangement of stones that is excellent for receiving libations is three tall or vertical stones arranged in a triangle with a stone slab placed on top like a table. The top stone should be a natural slab such as that found in some river beds, not a cut stone.

Sanctuary gardens need not be large at all, and the arrangement of stones can appear as just an inconspicuous accent in the corner of your yard. A sanctuary garden, however, is more effective if it is partially enclosed or its boundaries are defined in some way, as with a hedge or a fence of natural material. Groves, on the other hand, define themselves. For the indoor gardener, too, arrangements of stones among potted plants can become a sanctuary or a shrine.

If room permits and the area is private enough, it is also possible to arrange a garden that is an outdoor working Circle. All that is required is a bit of lawn in the proper diameter (nine feet is traditional) surrounded by shrubbery or a fence. A circle of stones can be placed around the perimeter, but this need not be a reproduction of Stonehenge—just four large, natural standing stones marking the four cardinal directions and the four Great Sabbats, and four smaller stones marking the cross quarters is sufficient. These stones can be tastefully arranged with shrubbery so as not to raise questions. An altar in the center need not be permanent, and a few bricks surrounding an earthen fire pit might be convenient.

Another idea for a garden, popular since the 14th century, is the garden maze. These elaborate pathways, which wind in and out between tall, sculptured hedge plants such as yew or boxwood, were designed as a form of entertainment for the upper classes, and they remained popular well into the 18th century. But they originated in the religious practices of the Pagan past. The footpaths of mazes were cut through the turf into the chalk of ancient England and were outlined by stones in the countries of Northern Europe. Unlike the mazes of later centuries in which one could easily become lost, these ancient mazes were one continuous path. Typically, the path began at the perimeter of the maze, spiraled in toward the center, then turned and spiraled outward again toward the perimeter. This is the spiral of the sacred dance still performed in some Pagan traditions at the Samhain Sabbat—the spiral dance that symbolizes death and rebirth. It is likely that similar dances were performed through the mazes at Samhain and again at Beltane, with which they are associated.

Similar mazes can be designed and incorporated into modern gardens on a smaller scale, and the sacred spiral dances can still be performed through them. Mazes can be planted of fast-growing privet or yew, a tree sacred in the Anglo-Saxon tradition. Both plants respond very well to severe pruning. Maze-like paths can also be planted in low-growing and easily pruned herbs such as the thymes, germander, or santolina. The sacred pathways of the spiral dance can even be worked in the stonework of a patio.

While it is the planting season, you might consider planting a tree or two for magical purposes. A rowan tree planted by the doorway protects against evil magic. A pair of maple trees planted in front of a house insures a happy marriage. (In the 18th and 19th centuries, when most houses were built facing south to take advantage of solar energy for extra heat, a pair of maple trees in front also provided shade in the Summer. They were known as Bride and Groom trees.) A hawthorn tree is sacred to faeries and may attract them. It is also a wishing tree. Both oak and holly are sacred trees, and in these days of indiscriminate destruction of forests, the planting of any tree can be seen as an act of worship of the old Pagan Gods.

This, too, is the time to begin planting a vegetable garden, and it is important to remember that many plants traditionally planted in the vegetable garden also have magical properties, and some are sacred. Potatoes are sacred to the Earth Mother and have several magical purposes, which will be discussed in a later chapter. Onions are sacred to both the Sun and the Moon, and they, too, have many magical uses. Lettuce is sacred to both the Moon and the element of Water, and string beans, because of their white flowers and sickle-shaped fruits, are sacred to the Moon Goddess. The tomatoes belong to the nightshade family and have

Offering a Libation in a Sanctuary Garden

many properties in common with nightshade, but tomatoes are a red fruit, and for centuries there was a taboo against eating any red food because it was considered fit only for the Gods. It was not until the 19th century that this ban on the tomato was lifted. Corn, of course, is sacred to the Grain Goddess or Earth Mother, as are squash, pumpkins, and gourds.

As you prepare the Earth to accept the seeds you are about to plant, it should be remembered that the act of plowing was a sacred act. It was a kind of sex magic between the farmer and the Earth Mother, in a time when men respected the Earth and the Goddess. And so whether you rake, rototill, or cut the furrows with hoe or digging stick, when the soil is prepared and before the seeds are planted, kneel down and spread your hands out over the soil and invoke the Goddess with words such as:

> *O Great Earth Mother*
> *We your adoring children invoke you,*
> *Grant us O Gracious One*
> *That you will accept the seed*
> *That we are about to plant in you*
> *That you may bring forth new life*
> *With which to nurture and sustain us.*
> *Blessed Be!*

The herb garden, where many magical herbs are grown.

Then begin planting the seeds that were blessed at the Vernal Equinox, either individually or by row or mound, and as you do so, chant:

> *Sprout leaf and root*
> *Bring forth fruit!*

April is the month during which followers of the new religion most frequently celebrate Easter, the resurrection of Jesus. The date of Easter Sunday is a moveable one and is placed on the first Sunday after the first Full Moon after the Vernal Equinox. Many of the Easter traditions popular today are of Pagan origin and are associated with either the Vernal Equinox or May Day.

The tradition of decorating eggs has already been discussed in the last chapter. Aside from Easter eggs, the most popular Easter symbol is the Easter bunny. Bunnies, be they rabbits or hares, are symbols of fertility because of their amazing rate of reproduction. For this reason they are associated with the fertility rites of Spring. But aside from the more obvious association with fertility, the rabbit has deeper meanings for the Pagan, and more obscure ones as well.

In the tin mining districts of England the rabbit was considered lucky, almost sacred, to the tin miners, who, like the rabbit, lived by burrowing into the Earth—the warrens of the rabbits resembling the tunnels of the tin mines. Rabbits seem to dwell in two worlds—this one and the underworld. For this reason, too, rabbits are associated with the fertility rites of Spring, when such ancient Pagan Gods and Goddesses of resurrection as Persephone, daughter of Demeter, Dionysus, son of Zeus, or Attis, beloved of Cybele, return from the underworld, bringing with them renewal of life to the Earth and a promise of eternal spiritual life to their worshippers.

The rabbit also is the medieval alchemical symbol for tin. Tin is a basic ingredient of bronze, which predates the use of iron by man by a few thousand years. It is brittle and rapidly rusts away by itself, but it gave to soft copper the strength and durability of bronze that was not surpassed until the Iron Age. Today, some Pagan traditions forbid the presence of iron in the Circle. This might suggest that the tradition dates to a pre-Iron Age origin (ca. 500 B.C.E.).

Tinsmiths, also called tinkers, may have worked magic and retained its secrets longer than practitioners of other crafts. That their powers were at one time legendary is suggested in the phrase, "a tinker's damn (curse)." Since tin is a white metal, tinkers are also known as white smiths, which clearly separates the tinker from the blacksmith, or worker of iron. This suggests a link between the white smith and the elves of Nordic mythology, and between the blacksmith and black dwarves. Elves are the "shining white ones" who influence humanity with their knowledge and ancient lore; black dwarves are the forgers of shapes that will manifest in the material world.

Tin also is sacred to the White Goddess, and so it is symbolically connected to the time of the Vernal Equinox, when the light half of the year begins to gain strength over the dark half, and the Lady once again steps forward.

The association between tin and rabbits is evident once again on several churches in Devon, England, which possess roof ornaments known as tinner's rabbits. These triangular carvings depict three sitting rabbits facing in different directions, all joined at the ear. A perfect symbol of the Triple Goddess. These Tinner's Rabbits bear a stunning resemblance to the highly collectable antique molds used to make chocolate Easter bunnies—molds which, incidentally, are made of tin.

Closely related to rabbits are hares, which are much larger than rabbits, with longer legs and ears, but hares do not burrow. In the legend of Cerridwen, after Gwion received the brew from the cauldron and was pursued by Cerridwen, he shifted his shape into that of a hare. Folklore abounds with stories of women accused of Witchcraft changing into the shape of rabbits or hares to escape their pursuers, and later, after assuming their own shape again, being exhausted or wounded as the hare was exhausted or wounded.

The March hare is not a particular species of hare but a condition of the common hare. The phrase "mad as a March hare" is closely related to "mad as a hatter," and predates Lewis Carroll and *Alice in Wonderland* by a few centuries. It is not clear what the meaning of "mad as a hatter" might be, but "mad as a March hare" refers to the excited and aggressive state of the hare during the mating season, which is in March. During Chaucer's time, "mad as a March hare" was a euphemism for sexual excitement.

So the chocolate Easter bunny is an ancient Pagan fertility symbol, and is spiritually appropriate at this time of the rebirth of Nature because, as one man put it, "The life of man is bound to death by way of reproduction." It is through sexual reproduction that we are born to experience the initiations of this life and the ultimate initiation of physical death so that we may be reborn again.

As the Hare Moon of April waxes full, observe the rabbits leaping and playing, carefree in their mating and joyful in their games, and as you cast your Esbat Circle and joyfully dance the round, feel within your heart the carefree nature of the wild creatures that are also the children of the Old Gods.

There can be little doubt that at this time of year sex magic, for a variety of reasons, was performed. And it is important for us as Pagans to

Offerings to the Goddess—a small altar in the woodland sanctuary garden

remember that when we recount examples of so-called fertility magic, we are often guilty of thinking that Pagans of old really believed that performing ritual sex in a cornfield actually made the corn grow. This is not necessarily true, and our Pagan ancestors were not the naive idiots that some would have us believe they were. In fact, they were the inventors of writing, mathematics, astronomy, medicine, metallurgy, agriculture, and civilization itself. They were not morons who put two and two together and came up with seven, but wise and knowing people who realized that when fertility magic, or ritual sex, was performed, a tremendous amount of psychic energy was released and that this energy could be directed by the will of the practitioners to make the corn grow, if that is what was desired.

In ancient times, this also was the time of year that a figure of the Goddess was carried or drawn around the countryside so that she could spread her life-giving blessings over the land. This figure of the Goddess was not venerated as the Goddess Herself, nor was it considered to be a likeness of the Goddess; it was a vehicle for Her spirit when she was invoked, so that Her priests were able to know when She was present. As priests drew the wagon or chariot bearing the figure of the Goddess, no doubt it was followed by bands of worshippers. This is possibly the origin of Easter parades. In ancient Egypt there were many such processions throughout the solar year, and figures of the Gods were taken from one temple to another. Today, in Mediterranean countries these processions are still being held, accompanied by celebrating and feasting. The ancient Pagan Gods have been disguised as saints of the new religion, but the message is the same: the God/Goddess has returned and by worshipping Him/Her, we are promised eternal spiritual life.

Many of the foods traditionally eaten at Easter are Pagan in origin. In some countries, tansy cakes were traditional Easter morning fare. The leaves of tansy are most often used for flavoring, although they have a mildly toxic effect that can accumulate; but it is probable that a tincture of the yellow, buttonlike flowers originally was used for the yellow dye they yield. This yellow dye would give to the cakes the color symbolic of the returning Sun. In other countries tansy-flavored omelets were eaten, combining the magic of the herb with the Sun symbolism of the eggs.

In Italy whole brown, white, or colored eggs are baked into braided loaves of bread to be eaten Easter morning, and during the Jewish celebration of Passover, eggs and sometimes a tincture of saffron give their golden color to the braided loaves of challah.

In Russia and the countries of Eastern Europe, a cheese dish called pashka is served with babka, an egg bread. Pashka is made by pressing cream cheese, cottage cheese, sour cream, and sweet butter through a sieve and whipping it with sugar, vanilla, and grated lemon peel. Then it is drained in cheesecloth in a flowerpot. On Easter morning the pashka is turned out and adorned with candied violets, and people greet one another with the phrase "He is Risen" as they partake of the violet-bedecked pashka. They are referring to the god of the new religion, of course, but the violets link the pashka to Attis, from whose blood violets sprang, and whose resurrection, after three days of mourning and ritual, was celebrated at the Vernal Equinox.

This widespread practice of eating bread made with eggs at this time of year, sometimes adding a golden color obtained from herbs, suggests an origin that combines the concept of the return of the Sun God with the return of the God or Goddess of Grain. It also suggests a ritual partaking of the physical body of the God.

One last tradition that must be mentioned here is the Easter basket. Even today, with the blessings of the new religion, it is filled with Pagan symbols, colored and decorated eggs, chocolate rabbits, marshmallow chicks, and confections of all sorts. The origin of the basket itself may be closely linked to eggs because it is believed by some that the earliest people were inspired to weave baskets by watching birds build the nests in which they laid their eggs.

In many European countries children went about on May Day begging gifts, much like our Halloween "trick or treat." The gifts given were often fruits or confections, and the children sometimes accompanied a pair of children who were King and Queen of the May, a couple who in ancient times represented the God and Goddess in a symbolic sacred marriage.

As April draws to a close, the brilliant golden yellow of daffodils and forsythia give way to pink azaleas, which range in color from red to white. Spikes of purple ajuga cover the ground above the bronze foliage. The lilac bushes are laden with heavenly perfumed purple or white blossoms, and the fruit orchard is a spectacle of flowers. The Easter basket is in fact the May basket about to be filled with the spectacular beauty of Nature in full bloom.

May

May

Most of the month of May could easily be spent just gazing into the woodland garden. There is an amazing variety of color and shape of flower in bloom. There are the brown and green stripes of the jack-in-the-pulpit, the nodding crimson crowns of the rock columbine, the bold white triangles of trilliums, the startling cerulean blue of Virginia bluebells, the secret hidden blossoms of wild ginger, and the lacy whiteness of saxifrage and foamflowers. Tightly coiled spirals of fern fiddles are beginning to emerge everywhere, and above all, the woodland sanctuary is filled with Nature spirits and flower faeries, which are especially active at this time of year.

As children many of us were able to see them. If we sat perfectly still in the forest where wildflowers were in bloom, eventually, and without warning, they would emerge from the plants themselves to play and laugh with one another. These tiny creatures appeared to be half human and half plant, not unlike the illustrations in the English "Flower Fairy" books of the Edwardian era (which, incidentally, I never saw until I was an adult, not having seen a real faery in almost 20 years).

It is my opinion that the human part of their appearance was contributed by my own consciousness as a sign that they were, like me, Spirit, and that the flower part of their appearance was a product of their self-awareness, because reality is as much what is projected as what is perceived. In other words, the flower faeries I saw were my perceptions of the astral bodies of wildflowers that had slipped out to frolic from the physical bodies of the plants as they dozed in the dappled light of the forest floor.

You may no longer see faeries, but you can still catch their movement or sense their presence. And so during the month of May, when they are most active, leave them little gifts in the woodland garden or on the forest floor. They especially like "fun food" such as cookies and soda.

In preparation for the May Day celebration, the bundle of wood for the Beltane Fire containing three pieces each of nine different kinds of wood was gathered in March. It is now quite dry and will give a fine blaze. You may wish to adorn it with white wildflowers or fruit blossoms and streamers of white ribbon in honor of the Goddess. As you bind the bundle of wood with ribbon, tying in the flowers, chant something like:

> *Bundle of wood with ribbons bound*
> *With flowers of white the Lady's crowned.*
> *Bundle of wood for the Beltane Fire*
> *Blaze and burn as I desire.*

These words may be repeated when you place your bundle of wood on the Beltane Fire.

Another traditional part of the May Day celebration is the May Bowl. By the first of May, sweet woodruff is in full bloom in the herb garden, its tiny clusters of fragrant white blossoms atop the carpet of hay-scented whorls of leaves. Sweet woodruff has no other use except as flavoring in May Wine. It does not cure or conjure or curse, but its exquisite scent, its pure white blossoms, and its habit of blooming on May Day make it an herb sacred to the Lady, and for that reason alone, it deserves respect and a good-sized space in the shadiest corner of the herb garden.

To prepare a May Bowl, place a few blossoming sprigs of woodruff in a glass punch bowl and pour over it a bottle or two of white wine and a cup or two of strawberry wine. (A wineglass or two of strawberry liquor will do if you don't have strawberry wine.) Add sugar to taste. If they are available, add a handful of fresh strawberries. The May Bowl, with white blossoms, green leaves, and red strawberries floating in crystal-clear white wine, is a visual treat, and its distinctive flavor when used for the Beltane rites year after year can induce that subtle shift in consciousness that is so vital to Pagan ritual.

As you fill your wine cups, drink to the Gods with words such as:

> *To the glory of May*
> *To our Lady and our Lord*
> *In perfect union*
> *And in perfect love*
> *Do we drink this Wine of May*
> *To the Gods!*

Pour libations of wine on the ground, or if your ritual takes place indoors, pour the libations into a cup or a bowl to be poured out in an appropriate place later.

The most popular and best-known May Day tradition is, of course, the Maypole. In Germany the Maypole was cut on May Eve by the young unmarried men of the village. It was of fir, and all of the branches except the uppermost were removed, as well as the bark. Then it was adorned with ribbons and erected in the village square, where it was guarded all night until the celebration of May Day morning.

Similar symbolism is found in the Osterfests, or Easter festivals, of Bavaria and Austria, where the poles are no longer surmounted by the tuft of evergreen but by the Christian cross instead. These poles are decorated with wreaths and hoops of evergreen and colored eggs, and are carried in procession to village churches, where they adorn the ends of pews as flowers would for a wedding.

In England, Maypoles were often erected well into this century at ancient sites such as the earthwork adjacent to the Chalk Giant of Cerne Abbas in Dorset. This 180-foot long figure was created by British Pagans, probably long before the sixth-century founding of a nearby Christian church, by removing sod to expose the white chalk beneath. This figure with its erect phallus leaves little doubt that it represents a god of fertility, and the equally phallic club it wields points directly to the earthworks where the Maypole was traditionally erected. A Maypole was erected annually at the great henge at Avebury well into the Victorian era as well. As in Germany, a fir tree was selected and cut in a nearby forest by young people and carried back to the village or sacred site where it was to be erected. Bound with red and white ribbons, the Maypole was about 80 feet tall, and some were much taller. One erected in London in 1661 was 134 feet tall.

One of the most important parts of the Maypole tradition is the round dance that takes place after it is erected. Dancers holding the ends of ribbons that are attached to the top of the Maypole dance around the pole in both directions—sometimes boys going one way, girls the other. As the ribbons wind around the pole and shorten, the round dance actually becomes a spiral dance, and with one group of dancers spiraling sunwise and the other group spiraling in the other direction, the dancing becomes an expression of death and resurrection.

The image of the Maypole—a fir tree with branches and bark removed being carried to the village or sacred site by a group of young men—is reminiscent of a scene depicted on the Gunderstrupp Cauldron, in which a group of men are portrayed carrying a tree trunk that has had the branches removed. They appear to be walking in procession, and the tree is being carried on the tips of their raised swords. Such tree trunks have been found in sacred wells used by the Druids to make offerings. These wells may have been considered openings to the underworld.

The Maypole, then, may represent the World Tree, with its roots in the underworld and its branches in the upper realms. It may be the Yggdrasil of Odin upon which he hung crucified for nine days and nights

Leaving an Offering for the Guardian of the Spring

until he sacrificed himself to his Self and received the sacred runes. It is also the tree trunk of the shaman, its top projecting up through the smoke-hole of the tent. It is along this tree trunk that the spirit of the shaman rides to the upper worlds of spirits or the lower world of the dead. This then may be the hobby horse of some May Day celebrations and the broomstick ridden by the Crone at Samhain. It is also the Tinne, the Glas-tin, the Tannen-baum, the Sacred Tree of Yuletide.

And like the fir tree adorned with fruits and flowers at Yuletide, the Maypole, bound around with ribbons of red and white, recalls again the rites performed by the priests and worshippers of the goddess Cybele. On the first day of the rites, a fir tree was bound with white woolen cloth like a corpse. Later priests and celebrants slashed their arms and sprinkled their blood on the altar of Cybele and on the sacred tree that represented her beloved Attis. On the fifth and final day, the Vernal Equinox, Attis is resurrected from the dead. The binding of the fir tree with white woolen cloth and the offerings of blood are recalled in the tradition of entwining the Maypole with red and white ribbons.

The Maypole is at once the venerated phallus and the World Tree. The connecting idea is that the spirit leaves the body and travels among the spirit realms via the World Tree during the shamanistic experience, the near-death experience, or that experienced through spiritual initiation and death. The spirit reenters a physical body after death and prior to rebirth via the phallus. So the phallus and the World Tree are two sides of the same coin, or two aspects of the God in his relationship to the Goddess in the endless cycle of birth, death, and rebirth.

For this reason the Sacred Marriage has been an important part of May Day celebrations in the past. The King and Queen of the May might have been at one time priest and priestess of the village, or a couple was appointed by them for having certain attributes. It is almost certain that the well-being of the community was dependent on the King and Queen's performance of ritual, which included sexual union. In some traditions the King and Queen of the May were instead called the Bride and Groom, and were accompanied by a wedding party of bridesmaids and groomsmen.

Today many areas still carry on the tradition of electing a May Queen, but the May King has been largely forgotten. In some areas the May King, or Jack-of-the-Green, was more important than even the May Queen. He was covered entirely with fresh branches of green leaves, with only a small opening for his face. In some traditions he also wore a headdress of leafy branches that made him appear taller than life. The type of branches most often used were birch or poplar, but sometimes fir was used, and in some cases holly and ivy. The Jack-of-the-Green is clearly the representation of the God of vegetation, and his mating with the Goddess as represented by the Queen of the May was a magical act that was necessary to the vigorous growth of the crops.

Another traditional activity for the month of May was the annual spring cleaning. It was during May that the temples of Rome were cleansed and purified. In England, part of this tradition was the cleaning of the chimney, and chimney sweeps were an important part of the procession that followed the Bride and Groom of the May and the Maypole. The chimney sweeps are especially associated with the Jack-of-the-Green. It is fairly certain that at some point in time the Jack-of-the-Green was the god of death and resurrection as personified by the village priest. His association with the chimney sweeps recalls testimony given at the witch trials of the 16th and 17th centuries concerning the mysterious Man in Black, which is discussed in a later chapter.

In spite of the fact that sacred marriages were performed in May, it was considered unlucky to get married during that month. This is probably because the lovely month of May, like red fruit, was considered fit only for the Gods. It is probably why, too, the following month of June is the traditional month for marriage between ordinary mortals.

It is traditional at May Day celebrations for women to wear chaplets of flowers on their heads. At this time of year the apple and pear trees are in bloom, and the tender branches, with leaves, blossoms and buds, lend themselves beautifully to being bent and tied into a crown. You may also wish to recall the role of the May King, or the Jack-of-the-Green, by making a crown of birch or poplar for the priest or any men who will share in your May Day celebrations.

Making and exchanging wreaths of flowers or foliage also is a very old tradition, and these wreaths were kept as amulets from May Day until June, when they were placed on the Midsummer Fire or in sacred groves or sanctuaries.

The term "Maying" refers to celebrating all of the traditions of May Day, and for that matter, of the entire month of May. It was traditional up until fairly recently to go on outings and picnics in the woods and meadows to enjoy the beauties of Nature, to pick flowers and to make love.

Picking May baskets full of flowers to be given or exchanged was a popular pastime that should today be confined to flowers grown especially for the purpose. Some of the flowers or plants picked in May had magical purposes. Cowslip picked before dawn on May Day and strewn about the house was a charm of protection.

Hawthorn, also called May bush because it blooms at this time of year, is sacred to the Goddess. Its pinkish white flowers, called "the May," were gathered for their purifying powers and hung about the house and on doorways as a protection against evil magic. The hawthorn is a favorite tree of faeries, and certain ones were considered sacred.

In England today, there still exists in a few communities a custom whose origins stretch back through the years to the time of the Druids. Well Dressing, as this custom is known today, is said to have started in 1349 when the village of Tissington was saved from the plague because of the purity of its water. As the custom is practiced today, scenes from the Bible are reproduced in entirely natural plant materials: flowers, leaves, herbs, mosses, lichens, etc. are set in clay on a wooden frame. These creations are cast into streams or pools during the month of May with the blessings of the Church as a thanksgiving for water. The custom is a recent echo of the ancient Druid festival of the Blessing of the Streams, during which garlands of flowers were cast into the water as a rite of purification. Wells, pools, and streams were held sacred by ancient Pagans, and throughout much of Europe such places have been found to contain offerings of anything from coins and wooden amulets to victims of human sacrifice.

To the ancient Romans, too, it was the custom to leave votive offerings at pools, wells, and fountains. Hundreds of gold coins and other artifacts have been discovered at Bath, England, where they were left as offerings to Sulis Athena. The famous Trevi Fountain of Rome, where thousands of tourists every year toss in a coin to make a wish, was originally a spring sacred to the Goddess Trivia, a Goddess of the Three Ways who is one more version of the Moon Goddess. And obviously, these ancient traditions are the origin of the "wishing well."

If there is a spring, well, or pool from which you collect water for ritual purposes, it is recommended that you become acquainted with the guardian spirit of the well. This spirit, usually invisible, can take any form—a newt or a damsel fly, for example. It is this spirit that maintains the magical power of the place and its waters. Communicate with the spirit on the inner planes, and always leave a gift or token in the pool, a coin or a flower in place of the water taken, with words such as:

> With grateful thanks I leave this gift
> For the Guardian Spirit of this well.
> For the water I have taken
> May it aid me in the sacred rites.

To represent that element on our altar, we collect water from a certain spring that flows from between rocks on a ledge overlooking the Delaware River. This spring is believed locally to have health-giving properties, and many people get their drinking water there. Although we've never encountered anyone when we have gone to get our water, we are always pleased to note that the rocks around it are kept clean and whitewashed, and although it is only a few feet from the road, it is kept free of the litter of picnickers and fishermen. We like to think it is the guardian of the spring that maintains it so nicely.

Even if you do leave a token at the well or spring each time you take water from it, it is especially nice during the month of May to bless the place of magical waters with a small bunch of flowers or herbs, or even to make it a point to visit several places—magical wells, deep mysterious pools, swift streams, and powerful cascades—leaving a floral offering at each and taking nothing in return.

This time of the Sacred Marriage of the God and Goddess is the Dyad Moon, the time when the two become one, when all things meet their opposites in perfect balance and in perfect harmony. As you cast your Circle this night of the Dyad Moon, adorn it with apple blossoms, and light candles of white. When the sacred round has been danced, sit a moment and reflect. Seek harmony in all things. As the dark half of the Wheel of the Year balances the light, as heat balances cold, recall the words of the Goddess, "Let there be beauty and strength, power and compassion, honor and humility, mirth and reverence, within you." And then before the rite is ended, if it is appropriate, become one with your working partner, physically as well as spiritually.

The month of May is one to enjoy from beginning to end. Nature is in full bloom, and the blossoms are the promise of a bountiful harvest to come. Taste the sweet wine of May, and gaze at the profusion of wild-flowers. Linger in the woodland glen and fern-filled glade and perhaps catch a glimpse of the bright elfin folk who dwell there. Spend quiet time by a sacred well or gaze into the depths of a mysterious pool. Scry the reflective surface of a pond, and bless the iridescent damselfly that seems to hesitate before you then disappears. Dance the round dance with joy in your heart, and rejoice with Demeter and Persephone as the Maypole is entwined.

June

June

The sunny days of early June are "hay-making weather." The warm, dry breezes are laden with the exotic, erotic fragrance of honeysuckle and wild rose. It perfumes the mornings filled with bird songs, the sunlit afternoons, and mingles with the scent of new-mown hay at night. In the woodland garden, after the spectacular variety and display of May, only one flower blooms now, the showy lady's-slipper orchid.

Spikes of white or fuchsia foxglove nod in the herb garden behind the ring of lavender chive blossoms that surround the beehive in the center. Clusters of purple lavender flowers dot the dusty gray plant, and the flat, yellow flower heads of rue stand in bright contrast to the blue-green foliage. Many culinary herbs are ready to be gathered now. The chipmunk that lives in the stone wall behind the herb garden pauses to look at us before disappearing into the labyrinth that he shares with some deer mice and a fat black toad.

This is a busy time for the birds who are feeding their growing broods. The big maple tree by the smokehouse is host to a colony of grackles. In Autumn, falling leaves will reveal an amazing number of their nests in the uppermost tips of branches. The mating call of the grackle, about as melodic as a rusty hinge, is quiet now that there are young in the nests. Lower in the same tree a robin feeds her hungry brood with insects gathered within feet of our back door. Another robin nests in the blue spruce at the back of the garden, and a pair of purple finches, brilliant in their courting plumage, are in the hemlock by the livingroom window. An oriole nest hangs over the herb garden, and the mockingbirds are in the vineyard, while the red-winged blackbirds weave their lovely baskets in the tall grass in the meadow. Catbirds, always the last to arrive, conceal their nests in the tangle of vines that have overgrown the hedgerow, but they feed in the herb garden and perch on the rain barrel. And the wrens have returned to their tiny house in the pear tree.

As the young of all these species of birds are hatched, their parents are

A Charm of Feathers and of String

busy carrying the empty eggshells far from the nest site to deceive predators who look for such telltale signs. So this is the perfect time to gather these shells for magical purposes. All bird eggs symbolize new beginnings. According to some, the universe itself began with the hatching of the Cosmic Egg. The type of bird and the color of the eggshell determine what sort of beginning activity is symbolized.

Robins are the very essence of Spring and have long been the symbol of the new year, and so their heavenly blue eggs are used simply for "new beginnings."

Grackles nest in large colonies, and so their pale blue eggs lightly speckled with brown can be used for magic that concerns any project involving a group of people.

The house wren is one of the most industrious of birds, sometimes building and maintaining two nests at a time, so its tiny white egg speckled with red-brown adds magic to any project involving hard work and industry.

The mockingbird is famous for its song. It does not actually imitate other bird songs, but it has such a varied repertoire of its own that it can vocalize for hours and sound like a whole forest of songbirds. Its light green egg clouded with blurry spots of brown should be worn or carried when it is necessary to do any public speaking, or as a magical aid to singers.

The little brilliant yellow goldfinch is a migratory bird, constantly following the ripening of thistle, dandelion, and milkweed, and so its tiny pure white egg is a charm to be carried on a journey, particularly one that is a quest.

There are literally thousands of species of birds in North America, and it is not the intention of this book to be the magical version of the Audubon Society's guide to the birds of North America. Instead, may it inspire you to observe the behavior of birds that live around you and to know that the shells of their eggs have the magical ability to transmit these characteristics or virtues.

If you are fortunate enough to find a hatched eggshell, this in itself should be considered a sign of favor. The eggshells can be collected and stored until they are needed. To take advantage of their magical properties, on the night of the New Moon add the appropriate type of eggshell to a small cloth bag of the correct color, along with herbs, stones, and other objects suited to the same purpose. Remember never to take a viable egg from a nest. This would not only violate a federal law that bans the collecting of bird eggs but would also violate the much higher law of "harm none" as well.

In Celtic countries, the characteristic behavior of birds aside, certain birds are associated with certain trees in the Celtic Tree Alphabet: the duck with rowan, the gull with alder, the crane with hazel, the hen with apple, etc. Symbolic designs representing these birds have the same meaning as the tree itself.

After the nesting season most birds molt their old feathers, making way for the new feathers that will carry them back to their Winter feeding grounds far to the south. This, then, is the time to collect feathers for use in magic later on. Like eggshells, feathers combine the characteristics of the bird with the magic of the color.

Red feathers symbolize physical vitality. The red feathers of the cardinal give the kind of physical vitality that enables these birds to survive Winters without migrating. The red feathers of the macaw, on the other hand, give the kind of sexual vitality that spawns the infinite variety of life that is the essence of the tropical rainforest, which is this bird's domain.

Blue feathers give mental abilities, peace, and protection. The feathers of the bluebird give more peace than those of the bluejay, which is noted for its noisy and aggressive behavior. But the bluejay that warns of the approach of an intruding cat gives protection in the form of psychic awareness.

Yellow feathers give cheerfulness and mental alertness, as well as prosperity. The yellow feathers of the canary give the cheerfulness of its song.

Green feathers give prosperity, growth, and health, especially the green feathers of tropical parrots and parakeets.

Brown feathers give stability and respect. Those brown feathers that are barred with black, like the tail feathers of the pheasant, give a balance between physical and spiritual life. Feathers that are banded brown and white or are half brown and half white give the kind of protection that enables you to go unnoticed among those that would harm you.

Black feathers, like the color black itself, are sometimes thought of simply as symbolizing negativity, evil, and death. But in fact they give the mystical wisdom that comes with true spiritual initiation, whether it is an initiation of symbolic death and rebirth of the spirit, or the wisdom that is gained through a series of actual physical lives, deaths, and rebirths.

Some black feathers, such as those of the grackle, are iridescent, flashing green and purple in sunlight. These give mystical insight. Feathers that are barred black (or gray) and white, like those of barred rock chickens, or spotted black and white like the guinea fowl, give balance and harmony.

Some feathers have very specific patterns or shapes, and these have very special magic. The most notable of these, of course, are the iridescent blue and purple "eyes" of the peacock's tail. These can be carried as a protection against the "evil eye," or worn on a headband to help in developing the third eye, or inner clairvoyant vision.

The rooster of certain breeds of chickens have on the center of their tails two feathers that are called sickles because of their long, curved shape. These feathers are the symbol of the God and the Goddess at once. They are sacred to the God because of their resemblance to the curved horns of many male animals and also because they are from only the rooster, itself a symbol of male virility. They are sacred to the Goddess because, as their name implies, they resemble the tool with which grain, sacred to Her, is reaped and also because they (and sickles) resemble the waxing and waning crescent Moon. Generally, white sickle feathers are sacred to the Goddess, and black ones, often iridescent, are sacred to the God. They can be worn as centerpieces for headdresses, as substitutes for the whole birds that were once worn by priests and shamans.

Feathers have long been used for ornament because of their beauty as well as their magical power. The natives of Papua, New Guinea make themselves elaborate headdresses from selected feathers of the many species of the spectacular birds of paradise. These headdresses not only impart their beauty to the wearer but they also magically impart certain characteristics the birds are noted for. The Indians of North America wear headdresses of eagle feathers both as a display of their courage and because the feathers magically impart this virtue. They consider feathers a gift from the Great Spirit. The Indian priests and chiefs of South America held the tail feathers of the quetzal sacred above all others. The birds were captured and their tail feathers plucked, and then the birds were released unharmed. The crime of injuring a quetzal was punishable by death. Shamans of many cultures wear feathers tied to their ritual robes or to the staff that is the symbol of their priesthood.

One of the most powerful charms that includes feathers is the Witches' Ladder. This is a cord made of three lengths of colored yarn braided together, with different colored feathers knotted into the cord at regular intervals. Witches' Ladders can be of two varieties—a general charm of protection and good fortune, or one for a specific purpose, such as the gaining of mystical knowledge, health, or prosperity. An all-purpose Witches' Ladder would include nine feathers, each of a different color, and a cord of three colors braided together. Three appropriate colors are white, red, and black, which represent the three aspects of the Goddess. A Witches' Ladder for a specific purpose would include three feathers and one length of yarn braided into the cord of a specific color.

To make a Witches' Ladder, gather together the necessary materials, preferably on the night of the Full Moon. Arrange an altar and cast a Circle. Take about a yard (three times the length of your arm from elbow to tip of little finger) of each color yarn, and tie the three ends together in a knot. Then begin braiding them together, chanting as you braid:

Yarn of Red, Black, and White
Work your magic spell this night.

Repeat this chant over and over until the entire length of yarn has been braided. (Braiding itself is a magical act because it makes three strands into one, representing the three aspects of the Goddess in one.) When the braid is finished, tie a knot in the end. Then starting about a foot from the beginning of the braid, tie the first feather with a knot around its base, saying (for a green feather):

With this feather and this string
Prosperity this charm will bring.

When all nine feathers have been tied into the cord as evenly spaced as possible, tie the ends of the cord together to form a circle. Then pass it through the candle flame and incense smoke, and asperge it with salt and water with words such as:

In the names of the Goddesses
And the God
By Air, Earth, Fire, and Water
I consecrate this charm
Of feathers nine and cord of three
As I will, so mote it be!

Then hang the Witches' Ladder high in your house, where it will not be seen by others who might be prejudiced toward it, but where you will see it every day.

Before there were fountain pens and ballpoint pens, there were quill pens, and some people today still prefer to use quill pens for writing charms and spells and for making talismans. Cutting the tip of a large wing feather with a penknife to make a pen is easy enough, and in mid-June a walk around a pond or lake where geese congregate can supply some fine goose quills for this purpose. Pure white goose quills make the best all-purpose pens, but for those magical processes that are the domain of Hecate, a black quill is more appropriate, and that of a black hen is perfect.

Feathers have been used in harmful magic, too, and finding a crown, a ring, or a cross of feathers in your pillow may be a sign that someone is working magic against you. One way to avoid this is to sleep on foam rubber.

One of the nicest things about feather magic is that there are so many interesting places where they can be found: ponds and lakes, pet shops, zoos, aviaries, fields, forests, and poultry farms.

By mid-June the weather has changed. It has become hot and humid.

MAKING A MAGICAL PEN

STEP 1: REMOVE THE BARBS FROM THE QUILL UNTIL IT IS COMFORTABLE TO HOLD.

STEP 2: SCOOP OUT THE BACK OF THE QUILL AND REMOVE THE CORE.

STEP 3: CUT A TINY NOTCH ON THE FRONT OF THE QUILL.

STEP 4: CUT A SLIT ON THE FRONT OF THE QUILL FROM THE NOTCH DOWN.

STEP 5: CUT THE TIP OF THE QUILL TO FORM A POINT.

STEP 1

90

It is the time of year when the hottest part of the day is usually spent indoors, but the still, fragrant evenings can be spent outdoors enjoying a display of fireflies in the tall meadow grass.

It will be an evening such as this that a resident toad might make its presence known. Toads are wonderful little animals that almost seem to seek out human companionship. We have one (or a series of incarnations of one) that has sat at our feet like a faithful dog on many Summer evenings, year after year. The main item of a toad's diet is slugs, so they are a boon to any gardener. Should a toad seek you out, consider it a sign of special favor, and be sure to keep a bowl of water available for it all Summer.

In the woodland garden the lady's-slippers have faded, but the cohosh or snakeroot has suddenly sent up a six-foot stalk that will bloom for weeks. Cohosh, or squawroot as it is also called, is a wild native herb used for its effectiveness in "women's complaints." The root, which is gathered in October for drying, was used by Native Americans 200 years ago, and is still used by modern manufacturers of natural vitamins in PMS (pre-menstrual syndrome) remedies. Cohosh, which grows in forests, is also called fairy candles. The spikes of its white flowers, like wax tapers, are borne on tall, thin, almost invisible stems above the foliage. In the shadowy light of the forest they appear to be candelabra held aloft by invisible beings who weave in and out among the trees in an endless procession. Because of the whiteness of the flowers and association between the magic of its root and a woman's monthly cycle, this plant is sacred to the Goddess, and the forests where it grows are Her domain. If you pay a visit to such a place around the time of the Summer Solstice, leave an offering for the Nature spirits who dwell there.

The Summer Solstice marks the time of the year that the waxing Sun reaches its zenith on the longest day of the year. To symbolize this aspect of the Solstice Ritual, it is appropriate to hang a Sun symbol high above the altar. This can be almost any natural object that is round in shape and gold or yellow in color. A huge sunflower might do, for example. Another appropriate symbol is a solar wheel or solar disc, an equal-armed cross surrounded by a circle. The Circle represents the Wheel of the Year, and where the arms of the cross intersect the circle are the solstices and equinoxes. This Solar Disc can be made of natural materials, such as grape vine, and tied with gold cord. Bunches of gold or yellow flowers, and those that bloom at the time of the Solstice, are especially suited and can be tied at the five points where the arms of the cross connect. Streamers of golden ribbon can also be tied to these intersections. If these streamers are dyed with onion skin to obtain the gold color, the powerful magic of the onion, with its strong solar association, will be imparted to the Solar Disc as well.

Hang the Solar Disc high above the Midsummer altar, and if your ritual is performed indoors, then the following day it can be taken outdoors to be hung high in a sacred tree that shades and protects your home, as a talisman to grant the blessings of the Gods in the coming solar cycle. If you have a Solar Disc or Symbol from the previous year, it should be added to the Midsummer Fire. The Midsummer Fire is traditionally kindled with the friction of fir and oak. Lighting a fire by friction has long been unnecessary, but a bundle of both types of wood should be used as kindling for the Midsummer Fire.

There are many herbs to be gathered at this time of year, but two that are especially traditional to gather on Midsummer's Eve are mistletoe and St.-John's-wort. Mistletoe gathered at this time does not yet have berries and is used as an amulet herb of protection. St.-John's-wort is in full bloom now, and sprays of it are hung up over doorways or beds as protection, especially against any harmful magic that might be worked against you. It is also beneficial to toss some onto the Midsummer Fire.

This is the season of severe Summer storms accompanied by thunder and lightning. So it is a good time to collect rainwater that is charged with the power of the storm. The more severe the storm, the more powerfully magic the rainwater. The rain should be collected in a glass or porcelain container. This container should not be allowed to touch the Earth, or the energy will be grounded. This powerfully charged water may be stored from storm to storm, or during seasons when there are no thunderstorms. This water will add its special energy to herbal brews, and can be used for anointing or asperging in any magical ritual to raise, generate, or transmit power; however, water stored for any length of time should not be ingested.

June is also the time of year that the cicadas emerge. There are many species of cicadas, and they have different life histories, but they all have one thing in common. That is, the larvae hatch from eggs laid in the twigs of trees. They then turn into an insect form called a nymph, which exists in a dormant state underground for a period of time that varies from one species to the next. Some emerge annually, some in a few years, and the famous 17-year locust, after many years. After years underground the white nymphs emerge and crawl upward, and then another transformation happens. The skin of the nymph splits open down the back and a winged adult emerges, leaving behind an empty shell that is perfect in every detail.

During a "Year of the Locust," the first signs of this natural phenomenon begin to appear as early as March or April. To the observing eye, empty skins begin to appear here and there among the grasses or on the bark of trees. This sight becomes more common, until by late May every tree,

A Witches' Ladder hangs from a beam

A Solar Disc in the rowan tree—Summer Solstice

every grove, every forest rings with the whirring of their calls. These mysterious creatures, who hatch in the treetops and then descend into the Earth where they dwell hidden for many years, fly on lovely fairy wings for a few days before they die, and the cycle is begun again.

As they fly from tree to tree to disperse their eggs, great numbers of birds are attracted to partake of the abundant feast. By the end of June the last of the cicadas have laid their eggs. The trees and forests are once again silent, and the ground is littered with their lacy wings.

The creative practitioner of magic who gathered the skins of the nymphs earlier in the Spring now collects the wings. Because of the powerful symbolism conveyed by these natural objects, which are available so seldom, their magic is potent. They lend their potency to charms and spells dealing with things hidden and secret. The skin can be worn in an amulet bag, along with hazelnuts, when on a quest for magical knowlege. A skin can also be worn as an amulet when you attempt astral travel, because it represents the empty shell of the body that the spirit or astral body has left. But their most important symbolism relates to the Gods and Goddesses who, like Dionysus or Ishtar, descended into the underworld to later emerge transformed, and for this reason the skins and wings should be worn as amulets by those who seek the type of spiritual transformation that takes place during true spiritual initiation.

As the daytime skies of June are dotted with cicadas, so the June evenings sparkle with the light of fireflies. They must have been a source of great mystery to ancient people, just as their cold light is to modern science. Coldness and light at first seem to be a contradiction, but magically it is a manifestation of the coming together of the Teutonic polarities of fire and ice. To the eye of one who is skilled in perceiving symbolic meaning in Nature, it is obvious that fireflies almost always light while ascending.

As every child knows, a jar full of fireflies is a source of magic and mystery. Its magic is closely linked to the lantern of the Hermit of the Tarot cards. This living light is an excellent source of light for many forms of scrying, and a wonderful focal point for meditation. Wishes whispered to fireflies will be carried to higher realms, but for any of this magic to work, the fireflies must be released before dawn to carry out their own purpose in this world as well as our own.

After the spectacular flowers of May have passed and the bees have gathered their pollen and nectar, the hives are filled with honey that is waiting to be gathered. In ancient times much of this honey was made into a drink called mead by a fermentation process similar to that of making wine. The "Moon in June" is the Mead Moon. Mead has been considered to have magical and even life-restoring properties in many of the countries of ancient Europe, and it was the drink of many of the great heroes of legend.

The legendary figure Robin Hood, who is accepted historically as being a composite of several peasant leaders during the reign of King Richard I, is also generally accepted by Pagans as being one of us. One reason is that Robin was a popular Witch name, and also because he was always described as being dressed in green, symbolic of the Green Man of Sherwood Forest. Lincoln green, which is made from woad, the dyestuff used by the Picts of ancient Britain and the Druid priestesses, is also a color that symbolizes, historically, the Pagan peasanty. Among the articles robbed from the rich by Robin Hood are "met and met." This probably means meat and mead. In the myth of Odin, one of his quests is for the Poetic Mead of Inspiration, which he returns to the realm of the Gods where it belongs, but a few drops fall to Earth, and this may be had by any-one who can find them.

On the night that the Mead Moon waxes full, after the Circle has been cast and dancing done, fill the cup with mead (if it is available), sweet wine, or an herb tea sweetened with honey. Sip the sweet drink and sit quietly and make yourself a vessel ready to receive the inspiration of the higher realms. Become a mead cup ready to be filled, not with the brew of everday life but with the clear, bright liquid of illumination. Every time this ritual is performed, even if there are no immediate results, you are becoming a more perfect vessel for divine inspiration.

If the night of the Mead Moon is very close to the Summer Solstice, the results of this exercise can be very powerful. If the Mead Moon is full on Midsummer Night, then the priestess into whom the Moon Is Drawn should be prepared.

As the month of May was considered unlucky for marriage, it being the month for the Divine Marriage only, June was considered the luckiest of months to be married in. The entire lunar marriage month, besides being called the Mead Moon, was also known as the honeymoon.

The honeymoon is not the only wedding tradition that has a Pagan origin. Most of them do. Today the white wedding gown is believed by Christians to symbolize the purity and virginity of the bride, but it is more likely to have come down to us from the Pagan past in which the dubious virtue of virginity was not one to be venerated. Instead, white symbolizes the Goddess, especially in Her aspect of the Maiden—the God-dess of love and beauty and of playful sensuousness.

As a symbol of the vows that have been exchanged, the bride and groom usually exchange wedding rings. Of all the articles of jewelry traditionally believed to have magical power, the most common are necklaces and rings. Both are magic Circles. The ring, being magically charged during the wedding ceremony, has the power to bind true love. The ring is placed on the third finger of the left hand in the belief that a main artery ran from that finger directly to the heart—the organ of love. There are many today who believe that spiritual love originates in the chakra located nearest the heart.

One of the wedding customs that seems certainly to have a Pagan origin is "throwing the garter." In many European Pagan traditions a garter is the symbol of a Pagan priestess, and the number of buckles on the garter represents the number of covens she presides over. In some of these same groups it is also held that a coven priestess must be young and beautiful to represent the Maiden, and therefore be unmarried. Throwing the garter, then, may have been a way for a priestess to randomly and impersonally select the next coven leader from among the eligible maidens at her wedding. Somewhere down through the ages this tradition probably got confused with another method of achieving the same thing—throwing the bouquet; and now young men catch the garter, but there is no denying the symbolism implied.

Two other wedding customs are probably related to one another: the toast and cutting the cake. The toast is traditionally performed by the father of the bride, and this is fitting because wine, or champagne, due to its ability to induce an altered state of consciousness, is symbolic of the Spirit or male principle.

The cake, on the other hand, symbolizes matter, the female principle. It is associated with bread in this way. Cutting the cake is accompanied by specific ritual. Usually the bride and groom each place a hand on the knife. If it is a military wedding, the groom may use his sword to cut into the cake. The sword or knife being a male symbol, there is no denying the fertility magic intended here.

The wedding cake may have its origin in ancient Sumeria. The bakers of this land had dozens of recipes for cakes and breads and baked them in all sorts of shapes for magical purposes. The wedding cake in its present form bears a stunning resemblance to a ziggurat, a pyramidal tower with a small chamber at the very top. The ziggurat itself represented the place where Spirit and Matter—or Heaven and Earth—meet, a place between the two worlds. In this sacred chamber at the top of the ziggurat, the temple priestess in one of the holiest of rituals had intercourse with the God Enlil. Whether this intercourse took place on the physical plane with a priest into whom the God had been invoked or on the spiritual plane while the priestess slept is not certain. This Sacred Marriage, though, is the basis for some of the most obscene accusations made against Witches by the Church during the Inquisition and other persecutions. It is also recalled in every multitiered wedding cake with the little figures of the bride and groom on the very top.

At Italian weddings today, there is a custom that has very ancient roots. After the cake has been served, each guest is given a small net bag, often with a sprig of artifical lily of the valley and an imitation wedding ring tied around it. This bag contains sugar-coated almonds called confetti. (The almond is the symbol of the ancient Phrygian fertility God Attis, whose cult became very popular in Rome.) Many people keep these bags of confetti as amulets and do not eat them. A closely related custom is showering the bride and groom with rice following the wedding ceremony. Here the ancient fertility blessing is obvious, and in earlier times no doubt grains of wheat or barley were used.

A more obscure custom, but still one tied to ancient fertility charms, is the custom of the groom carrying the bride over the threshold on their wedding night. A threshold today is simply a board nailed to the floor across a doorway to separate the floor of one room from the floor of another. But the name tells us that at one time it meant much more. Apparently the threshold was a retainer placed at the doorway of the threshing floor to keep any of the sacred grain from being lost or spilled. In ancient times the threshing floor was a sacred place. Perhaps in ancient times, too, a couple spent their wedding night in this sacred place in order to receive, or more likely to give, the energy of their sex magic.

The warm, dry breezes of early June give way to heat and humidity all too soon. The Summer Solstice has been celebrated, and from now until Yule the days grow shorter. But this time of the waning Sun is also the time of greatest abundance. The baskets of strawberries already consumed are only the beginning of the promises of the Gods that are about to be fulfilled.

July

July

The heat and haze of summer afternoons, the buzz of the cicadas in the still, oppressive air, are sometimes interrupted by a sudden Summer storm. More often the roll of distant thunder brings no rain to relieve the heat or quench the parched vegetables. Leaves wilt in the afternoon heat. When rain does come, it is often in the form of a downpour with such pounding force that it bruises the leaves of growing plants, releasing the fragrance of a multitude of herbs into the warm, moist air.

This is the time of year when it is traditional to pay a visit to the seashore. And that is a perfect time to gather some natural materials that might be useful for magical purposes, for rituals, and for charms and talismans thoughout the coming year.

Sand that has been collected from between the tide lines—that powerfully magical area between two worlds that is sometimes dry land and sometimes ocean bottom—is a wonderfully potent addition to any magical operation involving ocean deities, especially when it is sprinkled around the working Circle to mark the boundaries of this "place that is not a place." And since the tides are controlled by the Moon, the intertidal zone is the particular realm of the Moon Goddess.

A bottle of seawater can be collected for anointing or asperging. A substitute for seawater can be made by adding marine aquarium salt to distilled water, but it doesn't have the potent magic of the living sea itself, the birth-water from which all life emerged. And for this reason seawater is especially useful in rituals concerning new beginnings, particularly when they are performed at the time of the New Moon.

All seashells of the order *Gastropoda* (i.e., snails) grow in a spiral and are therefore sacred to the Goddess. In many species the spiral isn't always apparent, but often shells found on the beach are broken to emphasize the internal spiral structure.

One genus of shells, the cowries, are particularly sacred to the Goddess because their slit-like apertures bear a strong resemblance to female

Gathering Magical Herbs with the White-Handled Knife

genitals. (A closely related species is called in Latin *Volva volva.*) For this reason, and because the shells are strikingly beautiful, they were left as offerings at the Temple of Aphrodite on Cyprus, from where the genus gets its scientific name *Cypraea.* And because shells of the genus *Cypraea* have a highly glossy smooth surface as well as a vagina-like opening, pregnant women in the South Pacific insured a smooth delivery by rubbing their abdomens with the shells.

Many snails have an appendage called an operculum, which works like a trap door sealing the opening of the shell when the animal has withdrawn into it. Operculums come in a variety of shapes according to their species, but those of the genus *Turbo* are amazing for their colors and decorations. Most have a clear spiral drawn on the flat interior surface, and the convex exterior might be red or brown or black, or decorated with white tubercles. Those of the *Turbo petholatus,* or Tapestry Turban of tropical waters, are a deep iridescent green and are called Cat's Eyes. These Cat's Eyes are sometimes set into jewelry and worn as amulets of protection against the evil eye.

The bivalves of the family *Pinnidae* are related to mussels, and like mussels these animals produce a thread. The large tufts of this thread called the *byssus* is attatched to rocks buried in the sand to anchor the pen shells to the sea floor. The fibers of the byssus of the pen shells are a rich brown with bright gold highlights, and in Mediterranean countries they were spun into a single length and woven into small articles of fine silk that sold at high prices. It is believed by some that the legendary golden fleece sought by Jason and his Argonauts for its magical and healing properties was in reality made of the byssus of pen shells, and anyone who has seen this lovely golden silk from the sea would probably agree. There are three species of pen shells in North America, and two are quite common.

Sand dollars are natural pentacles with their five-part radial symmetry forming a five-pointed figure in the center of a round white disc. These can be used as altar pentacles or worn as pentacles of natural shell jewelry. It is possible to arrange an altar entirely with objects found on the shore. When a sand dollar is broken open, parts of the internal structure will fall out. These parts look very much like miniature doves, and today they are said to represent the Holy Ghost of the new religion. No doubt in ancient times they were the sacred doves of Aphrodite.

One of the most treasured objects found on the beach (although they can be found in other places, too) is the Holey Stone, a stone or pebble with a natural hole in it. When such a stone is found it is appropriate to thank the Gods who left it there. Take the stone home and on the night of the next Full Moon cast a Circle according to your ways and sprinkle a circle of sand about the stone. Asperge it with seawater and hold the stone high with the fingers of both hands while reciting words like:

O Gracious Goddess
You have placed this Holey Stone
On my pathway for me to find.
Grant it now become a vessel
Of your divine power
To aid me in my magical work.
In your name Gracious Goddess
Do I consecrate this Holey Stone.

View the Moon through the hole in the stone and know that it is being charged with Moon magic. Then wrap it in a bit of white linen and place it in your amulet bag or wherever you keep amulets.

Feathers have a wide range of uses in magic, from Witches' Ladders to American Indian medicine fans, and the feathers of the seagull are especially potent because this bird is at home in three of the elements: Water, Air, and Earth. Seagull feathers can often be collected on the beach.

There are a number of nuts and seeds that can be found washed up on beaches. These have always been regarded as having magical powers by people around the world, from legendary Indian rulers to Scottish fishermen. The most famous of all these nuts is, of course, the coco de mer, which washes up on the shores of India. Its source, the Seychelles islands, was not discovered until the seventeenth century. It grows nowhere else, and was used as a medicine and an aphrodisiac because of its erotic shape. It is the largest nut in the world.

A coco de mer is not likely to wash up on the shores of North America, but there are several nuts that do, and they all carry with them the magic and mystery of far distant lands as well as the tradition of magical uses. The most common of these are the sea heart, the sea bean, and the gray nickernut.

The sea heart (*Entada gigas*) is a large, heart-shaped seed (about two inches in size) of smooth, shiny dark brown. In Norway, women in labor would drink a brew from a cup made of the seed case of the sea heart to relieve the pain. In England sea hearts were given as amulets to young men going to sea.

The sea bean (*Mucuna* sp.) is a lovely brown seed one inch in diameter. It is round and flattened with a black band outlined in cream that goes about three-fourths of the way around it. In western Ireland the sea bean was placed under the pillow at night to protect against mischievous spirits.

The gray nickernut (*Caesalpinia bonduc*) is a smooth, almost perfectly round, light gray nut ("nicker" is another name for marble) about one-half inch in diameter. In the Hebrides islands they are worn as protective amulets and are said to darken if the owner is in danger.

A visit to the beach is a perfect time to perform magic as well as to collect magical material. It will be necessary to consult a tide table to insure that the timing of your visit coincides with the purpose of the magic you plan to perform. An incoming tide and an increasing Moon are the time to weave spells of increase, prosperity, and fertility. An outgoing tide and a waning Moon are the time for banishing illness and troubles. But above all, the shoreline is the perfect place for us to express our love for the Gods, especially in their aspects as sea deities. In that magical place between land and sea at dawn or dusk, between night and day, cast your magic Circle in the sand, build a fire of driftwood, anoint yourself in the life-giving water, and pour libations of wine.

Once we've refreshed ourselves on the beach and recharged our psychic batteries in the surging power of the sea, we return to the rolling hills of our home in western New Jersey to begin the harvest.

The first major harvest from the garden is cabbage. When all the cabbage has been picked, we remove the outer leaves for stuffing and split the heads, aware of the Tree of Life design revealed within. Then we begin making saurkraut. This activity takes on the atmosphere of a festival as we slice the quartered heads of cabbages dime thin, weigh the shredded vegetable, add three tablespoons of salt to each five pounds of sliced cabbage, and take turns stomping it in an old crock until it is covered in its own liquid. This will ferment in the cellar until it is canned sometime during the waning Moon in September.

To celebrate the cabbage harvest, set aside one small but perfect head. This can be made into a bowl of coleslaw or other cabbage dish to be a major part of the Cabbage Harvest Feast. Set aside a small portion of this food on a plate along with an equal portion of last year's saurkraut. These represent harvests past and future; saurkraut represents food preserved for Winter, while the fresh cabbage dish represents Summer food; together these foods symbolize Nature's abundance that provides for both the dark and the light half of the Wheel of the Year. Carry the plate of "old" and "new" food to the cabbage patch in your garden, and using your athame, draw a Circle in the Earth, then draw a line dividing it in half. Bury the "old" food in one half and the "new" food in the other while reciting words like:

> As this Season of Plenty begins
> We give thanks to the God and Goddess
> For the food with which we are blessed
> And we ask you Lord and Lady
> To accept this token of our love.
> As darkness follows light,

So lightness follows dark,
In perfect balance and in all things
This is way of the mighty Gods,
Blessed be.

Then erase the drawing of the Circle on the ground.

As the Wort Moon of July waxes full, this is the time for the gathering of herbs. The word *wort* is old Anglo-Saxon for "herb." Among the magical herbs ready to harvest now is that most magical of herbs, vervain, so revered by the ancients for its hidden powers. (Magical mugwort, too, is ready to gather at this time.) The lavender spikes of vervain complement and contrast with the yellow of the goldenrod, and the candelabra-like shape of its flower stalk distinguishes it from loosestrife, with which it can easily be confused. The ancient Greeks used vervain to adorn their altars, and Druids in Britain included it in their rituals of prophecy. It can be used to decorate the altars of contemporary Pagans as well, and because it has strong associations with purity, it can be used with spring water to asperge the Circle or working area before rituals of purification, exorcism, or consecration. It is also useful to banish interference prior to divinatory rituals such as crystal gazing, Tarot reading, or rune casting. A dried sprig of vervain kept with a Tarot deck will keep one spread or reading from interfering with the next. It is also used in many love charms.

The time that an herb is gathered is very important, whether it is for a magical purpose or a culinary one. (Medicinal or healing herbs are considered magical.) If the aerial part of the plant is to be used, then the plant should be harvested as it is coming into bloom during a waxing Moon. In the case of some herbs this will stimulate a second or third blooming. If the roots or bulbs are to be used, the herb should be gathered during a waning Moon when first coming up, or after it has grown for a season and all of the foliage has died back down, returning the energy to the bulb or root. It is also important to gather magical herbs during the correct planetary hour and day of the week. Plants that are to be stored should be collected on a dry, sunny day.

The time an herb is gathered is not necessarily the same as the time it should be used magically. Vervain, for example, is most potent when gathered on a Monday or a Friday during a waxing Moon, as it is coming into bloom, but if it is to be used for a banishing ritual, this is best performed on a Saturday during a waning Moon.

Many occult herbalists and magical practitioners use a white-handled knife consecrated specifically for the purpose of collecting herbs and carving magical signs and symbols, etc. When approaching a plant about to be gathered for magical use, draw a Circle in the Earth using the white-handled knife. Then pointing the knife at the plant, draw an invoking pentagram and intone words such as:

> *O Spirit of Vervain I invoke Thee.*
> *Herb of Purity I beseech Thee.*
> *In the name of the Goddess Diana,*
> *Chaste and pure, accompany me*
> *And aid me in the ancient Craft.*

Then as swiftly and painlessly as possible, sever the desired branches or leaves, and still using the white-handled knife, dig a small hole in front of the plant and leave an offering—a coin or a piece of bread (nothing too sweet, because it could attract ants that might eventually damage the plant). A pinch of plant food is always appropriate.

Once the herb has been cut, it must not be allowed to touch the ground, or its magical properties will be returned to the Earth. For this purpose a white linen or cotton cloth or cloth bag or an herb-gathering basket is useful. An herb-gathering basket is one that is loosely woven to promote air circulation for drying the herb and preventing mold. Once the herbs have been gathered they can be used fresh or hung up to dry in a dry, shady place; an attic is ideal.

When the magical herbs have been gathered and hung to dry, the time of the Full Moon is the time to give thanks to the spirits who dwell in the herb garden, and to leave them an offering. Perhaps as you place an offering in the moonlit garden, they will whisper to you other secrets of herbal magic.

Later in the month, when all the plants have turned yellow and fallen over, the potatoes are ready to harvest. Dan gently turns the soil with a pitchfork while I follow him, my bare feet planted in the dirt, my fingers feeling in the warm, moist soil for the potatoes.

Potatoes are of the element of Earth. Their color, their taste, their smell, are of the Earth. In the dark moistness of Earth they grow, and in the cool darkness of the earthy cellar they must be stored, because if they are exposed to the elements of Air and Sun, their skins become the poisonous green of the nightshade family to which they belong.

Potatoes are amulets of Earth, and they may be used magically as well as eaten ritually. One way that a potato can be used magically is to carve its skin with magical signs, runes, or symbols expressing the result you wish to bring about, and then bury it in the Earth (or hide it in a cave). As the potato returns to the element of Earth it takes with it the secrets of your desire, which the Earth can then grant you. Potato Earth magic is

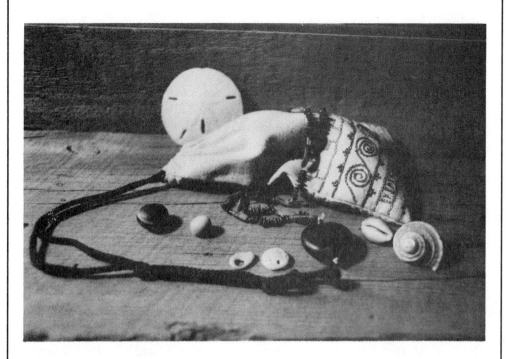

An amulet bag and magical objects found on the shore

A potato Earth Mother and potato-stamped harvest basket

especially potent in the areas of slow growth, prosperity, gradual increase, and secret power.

Another way of working magic with potatoes is to slice a potato in half, exposing a flat white surface. Magical runes or symbols can be carved into this surface, or the background can be carved away, leaving a raised rune or symbol. This can then be dipped in paint and used as a stamp to mark cloth, paper, or painted wooden surfaces. The resulting design will bear not only the magic of the symbol or rune, but the Earth magic of the potato as well. The colors should be Earth colors—dark reds, warm browns, and soft greens. I have used this method to mark harvest baskets and a tiny paper box in which I keep a very special and highly charged Earth amulet.

To celebrate the potato harvest, have a feast, a meal that features potatoes, whether they are baked in an open fire or sliced into a great potato salad. Afterward, select one potato from the harvest for its shape (or rather it will select itself), and after working the soil of the potato bed removing weeds and rocks, and adding a Winter feeding of bone meal and lime, carve the potato into the likeness of an ancient fertility Goddess, the Earth Mother. Rake the soil of the bed into a mound and bury the fertility figure deep in the very center of the mound with words such as:

> *O Great Earth Mother*
> *From whom we receive all nourishment*
> *And the flesh of our bodies,*
> *We your loving children*
> *Make this offering in your honor*
> *In love and in gratefulness*
> *Blessed be!*

By Lammas Eve, the last day of the month, our harvest is in full swing. We have tasted the abundance, we have eaten our fill of tomatoes and peaches and corn on the cob. We have begun to can tomatoes and pickle cucumbers, and the cellar is beginning to be filled with potatoes and saurkraut. We celebrate the Harvest Festival with whole grain bread and wine from last year's vintage. The Circle of our ritual is decorated with bowls and baskets of the harvest: tomatoes, potatoes, onions, and peaches. It is a time to give thanks and to celebrate.

August

August

The first weeks of August continue hot and humid. In the meadow a herd of dairy cows seek the shade of the trees that grow by the creek. Here and there in fields and along roadsides the first goldenrod begin to appear, splashes of deep yellow which hint at the blaze of color that will follow in the months to come. Elsewhere, Queen Anne's lace, like bits of tattered wedding gown, cover fields with delicate white, and the feathery fluffs of milkweed seeds burst from their pods to await the breezes.

In the woodland garden, where just a few months ago a great variety of flowers bloomed, now only seed pods dry and ripen. The berry clusters of Solomon's-seal are flush with pink, and the fruits of jack-in-the-pulpit, like nuggets of bright green jade, swell in their papery sheaths.

Much of the vegetable garden is finished now. The beds of earth have been turned and lie baking in the Summer sun. Crickets hide in the shade of squash leaves, creaking out their songs, and the startled grasshopper catapults itself to another blade of grass in the buzz of the Summer afternoon.

The month of August begins with Lammas, the celebration of the first harvest, especially the grain harvest. The sanctity of grain goes back almost as far as the human race itself. In southern climates the sacred grain is usually corn, rice, or millet; in northern climates, rye, barley or oats, and in temperate climates, wheat.

These grains, too, were associated with Gods or Goddesses of death and resurrection. The oldest possibly is Tammuz the Sumerian god, beloved of Ishtar. In the Sumerian myth, Tammuz is slain by another god and passes into the underworld, leaving the bereaved Ishtar. Because of their separation, all Nature ceases to function and reproduce itself. Finally the grieving Ishtar descends into the underworld to bring back her beloved consort Tammuz (presumably, as the text is incomplete).

To the Syrians, Babylonians, and Phoenicians the Grain God was Adonis. Adonis actually meant "lord" ("Adoni" in Hebrew), but it became

A Celebration of the Harvest

the name of this God to the Greeks. Born from a myrrh tree, the God Adonis became the beloved of Aphrodite, Goddess of Love (Astarte to the Phoenicians). Persephone, Goddess of Death, fell in love with him too, and the two Goddesses fought bitterly over him. The argument was settled by Zeus, who ordered that Adonis spend six months of every year with Persephone in the underworld, and the rest of the year with Aphrodite. In Phrygia (Turkey), this God is called Attis, and his beloved is Cybele. After his death by self-mutilation, he, too, is permitted by Zeus to return from the dead for six months every year.

In countries north of the Mediterranean coast, the grain deity is usually a female. In parts of Greece she was Demeter, whose daughter Persephone was loved by Hades, son of Zeus and lord of the underworld. He kidnapped her one day and kept her captive in his dark domain. Demeter, furious at Zeus for allowing this to happen, ordered the Earth not to bear fruits or grains until her daughter was returned. Seeing this, Zeus agreed that Persephone should be allowed to return to Demeter for eight months out of every year.

Ceres, from whose name the word "cereal" is derived, is the Roman equivalent of Demeter, and her daughter Proserpina is that of Persephone. They were referred to as the Two Goddesses, but are portayed as two aspects of a single Goddess.

In the Cyclades islands of Greece, highly stylized fertility figures with arms folded across the chest are found in many an ancient tomb. These figures are often found in pairs with one slightly smaller than the other, and both figures ritually broken in half. These figures no doubt represent Demeter and Persephone and are charms buried with the dead to insure their resurrection.

Some of the names applied to Demeter/Persephone are She of the Corn, She of the Threshing Floor, She of the Seed, and She of the Great Loaf. To the Anglo-Saxons and Norse people the Goddess Freyja is, among other things, a fertility or grain Goddess, and Her name means The Lady, or Giver of the Loaf. To the Celts She is Bride.

The practice of baking bread is probably almost as old as that of harvesting grain. It is a four-step process: grinding the grain, moistening it with water, shaping it into a loaf, and baking it. The use of yeast to cause bread to rise came much later, probably in Egypt, where they already used it for brewing beer and wine.

The first part of the process, grinding, was first accomplished by pounding the grain between two stones. Then the quern, a hand-operated pair of grindstones, was developed, which led directly to the gristmill with its huge millstones. The act of milling or grinding was thought of in some cultures as the destruction of the Grain God. The circular motion of the millstone with it spiraling grooves, dancing its rhythmic round dance over the grain, may have some connection with Caer Arianrod, Castle of Arianrod, or Castle of the Silver Wheel, a dwelling place of the dead. The Goddess Arianrod had a son Llew Llaw, a golden-haired boy who was remarkable for his rapid growth. He sometimes is considered a Sun God, but he is just as easily a grain or vegetation God, because one of his first feats is to kill a gold-crest wren, which associates him with the Oak/Holly King cycle. His mother Arianrod, the Silver Wheel, is the Goddess in her "Life in Death" aspect. Llew Llaw is finally destroyed though Blodeuwedd, The Flower Faced, or The Goddess in her aspect as Death in Life. But since Llew Llaw is a Grain God, he is also a God of death and resurrection. The sacred meal or grist that is the result of milling is so universal that in Tibet the barley meal which is a part of the daily diet is called tsampa, and the corn meal of the Indians of the northeastern United States is called samp.

It is said that every house in Chaldea had a grindstone and a bread oven. In the Eastern European countries of the Ukraine, Yugoslavia, Czechoslovakia, and Hungary are found small clay temple models that date to the neolithic period (6000–5000 BCE). These miniature temples, or shrines, contain several interesting features. Many of them have bird heads as a part of the architectural elements, indicating that they are

A loaf of ritually baked and blessed bread
and an ancient Phoenician fertility Goddess

shrines to the documented Bird Goddess of the area, and some of them have human figures shaping and baking loaves of bread in bread ovens. In these countries still known for their wheat, Siva or Ziva was the Goddess of Life, and was portrayed as holding a sheaf of wheat. These little shrines with their bird motifs recall at once both the small gold plaques with their sacred doves of the temple of Aphrodite found by Schleimann at Mycenae, and the Sanctuary at Paphos on Cyprus, where Aphrodite and Adonis were worshipped. There is an obvious connection between the scenes of sacred bread baking and votive bird figures of the Indo-European countries, between the sacred doves of Aphrodite and her consort the Grain God Adonis, and between Tammuz the Sumerian Grain God and his beloved Ishtar, who at times took the form of a bird. There was a grove of trees sacred to Tammuz/Adonis in Bethlehem, which according to Christian mythology was the birthplace of Jesus. (The name *Bethlehem* means "House of bread.")

If the harvesting, winnowing, and grinding of the grain is the death of the God, then the sprouting of the grain is his resurrection. For this reason women in some Mediterranean countries would ritually sprout seeds of grain in dishes or pots called Gardens of Adonis to be given as offerings— either thrown into rivers or later left at churches of the new religion. Since the grain—winnowed, ground, and ritually baked in temple ovens—is the body of the dying God, then eating this ritually baked bread is to partake of the flesh of the God. For this reason the loaves were sometimes baked in the shape of the human body.

Whether you call the God/Goddess of the Grain Adonis or Tammuz, Demeter or Freyja, or John Barleycorn, the baking of bread should be a sacred ritual, especially at Lammas. It is especially appropriate at this time to add sprouted wheat to the bread dough to express the idea of the dying and the resurrecting God of Grain. If you plan to do this, the wheat sprouts should be started a few days before bread baking.

This is one recipe you can use for whole grain bread for the Lammas Ritual:

In a large mixing bowl combine two cups of milk warm to the touch, two packages of dry baking yeast, one teaspoon salt, one-half cup of honey and one-fourth cup of dark brown sugar. Cover the bowl and set it aside in a warm place until it has doubled (about half an hour). Add to this mixture three tablespoons of softened butter and two cups of unbleached white flour, and stir until bubbly. This is the time to add the sprouted wheat if you wish.

Then mix in one cup of rye flour and two cups of stone-ground whole wheat flour. With floured hands turn this dough out onto a floured board and gradually knead in more unbleached white flour until the dough is smooth and elastic and no longer sticks to your fingers.

Place this dough in a greased bowl, turning it so that the dough is greased, then cover it with a clean cloth and keep it in a warm place to rise until it is doubled (about an hour). Then punch it down and divide it in half. Shape it into two round, slightly flattened balls, and place it on greased cookie sheets. Cover these and return them to a warm place until they double again.

When the final rising is almost complete, with your athame incise a pentagram on the loaf with words such as:

> *I invoke thee beloved Spirit of the Grain*
> *Be present in this Sacred Loaf.*

Beat a whole egg and a tablespoon of water together and brush this over the loaves. Bake the loaves in a 300° oven for about an hour, or until they are done and sound hollow when they are tapped.

By mid-month the heat and humidity are for the most part behind us. We have celebrated the harvest with the Lammas Feast. We begin to feel a sense of urgency to gather the harvest before the coming of Winter.

Onions that were planted in May and pulled in late July have been cured in the Sun every sunny day for at least two weeks. On the Full Moon, when the Sun is in Leo, the Wort Moon, we celebrate with onion braiding. Braiding onions is an ancient way of storing them. It is easy, fun, and magical.

Begin by doubling a yard of heavy twine in half and tying a knot so that the middle of the twine forms a loop. Lay the twine on a table in front of you so that the loop and knot are away from you and the two loose ends are toward you. Then take an onion in your weaker hand upside down and place the dried top that was the foliage just below the knot between the two lengths of twine so that the onion top becomes the center of three strands to be braided together. Crisscross the onion top with the twine twice "pigtail" fashion, then add a second onion the same way as the first and crisscross the combined onion tops twice with the twine. Repeat the process until there are only a few inches of twine left, and tie the two ends of twine together in a tight knot. Lift the braid of onions gently by the loop at the top, and it is ready to hang in the root cellar for Winter storage, or anywhere in the house as a charm of protection. Onion braids are especially useful in the sick room because they protect by absorbing negativity rather than repelling it.

To make an onion braid specifically as a charm, follow the same procedure as above except that it can be done within a Circle. As you rhythmically braid the twine and onion tops together, chant words such as:

> *Charm of Onions, Charm of String*
> *Evil to thine own self bring.*
> *Charm of Onions and of Twine,*
> *Thou shalt protect this house of mine.*

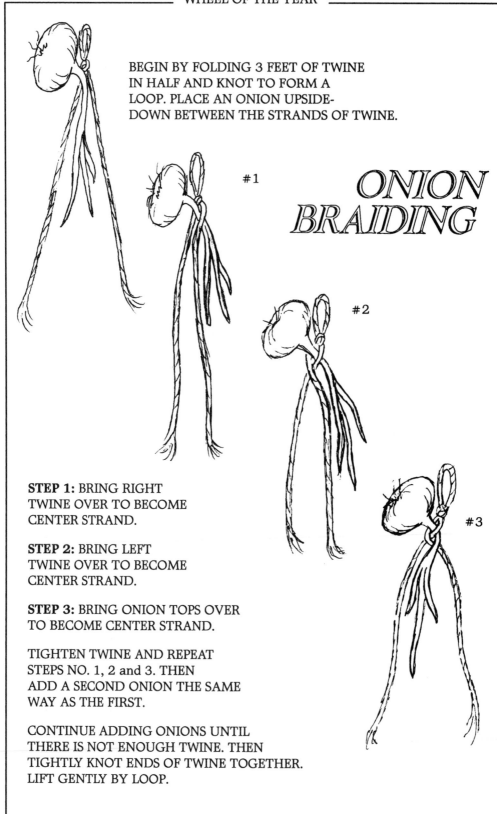

BEGIN BY FOLDING 3 FEET OF TWINE
IN HALF AND KNOT TO FORM A
LOOP. PLACE AN ONION UPSIDE-
DOWN BETWEEN THE STRANDS OF TWINE.

#1

ONION BRAIDING

#2

#3

STEP 1: BRING RIGHT
TWINE OVER TO BECOME
CENTER STRAND.

STEP 2: BRING LEFT
TWINE OVER TO BECOME
CENTER STRAND.

STEP 3: BRING ONION TOPS OVER
TO BECOME CENTER STRAND.

TIGHTEN TWINE AND REPEAT
STEPS NO. 1, 2 and 3. THEN
ADD A SECOND ONION THE SAME
WAY AS THE FIRST.

CONTINUE ADDING ONIONS UNTIL
THERE IS NOT ENOUGH TWINE. THEN
TIGHTLY KNOT ENDS OF TWINE TOGETHER.
LIFT GENTLY BY LOOP.

After a year onions begin to lose their protective powers because they don't last much longer than that, so the onion braid should be replaced annually.

The use of onions in magic is potent because of their complex but powerful symbolism. The globose shape of the onion, covered with its amber skin, is symbolic of the Sun, under whose rulership in Leo it is ready to harvest. When the skin is removed it yields a dye ranging from golden amber to burnt apricot. This dye can be used as an ink for inscribing Sun talismans or to dye handspun cords where the color is appropriate. It is also a perfect dye for eggs for the celebration of the Vernal Equinox (a bit of the skin in a pot of boiling eggs always lets you know which ones are hard-boiled).

When the onion is cut open it reveals the symbolism of the Moon. If it is cut horizontally it displays the white disc of the Full Moon, but if it is cut vertically it shows the east- and west-facing crescents of the waxing and waning Moon. Some onions, when cut horizontally, reveal a yin/yang design that repeats the duality of the Sun/Moon symbolism.

Garlic is another powerfully magic bulb that can be braided like the onion. Its papery white skin and crescent-shaped segments make it sacred to the Moon. The protective properties of garlic work more on a psychic level than on a physical one and should be used instead of onion when the cause of negativity is of a more psychic nature. The presence of a braid of garlic in the home exorcises it as well as protects it.

One day at mid-month we realize that the robins and wrens that were nesting nearby have simply vanished. Their lovely songs have been replaced by the shrill calls of the bluejays, who were so silent during the nesting season.

As August progresses the days are still hot but nighttime temperatures are beginning to cool, and the late afternoon thunderstorms that bring the cooler air also bring about the ripening of tomatoes. Every few days there is a basket or two to pick, and with an attitude of thanks we can six to a dozen quarts until we have reached our quota of 48 quarts, all the while eating fresh tomatoes with every Summer meal.

In the fields and meadows and along roadsides now there are wild herbs to be gathered. There are goldenrod, Queen Anne's lace, and milkweed—all awaiting the natural dyer who can extract from them tan, green, and bright yellow respectively, for dyes and for natural inks for talismans. Among the medicinal herbs to be collected at this time is boneset, which does not help broken bones to heal but is a febrifuge that

PLANT	COLOR	MATERIAL TO BE DYED	PART OF PLANT	MORDANT*
ONION	BRIGHT YELLOW, ORANGE, RUST	WOOL YARN EGGS	SKIN	ALUM ON WOOL
ONION	OLIVE GREEN	WOOL YARN	SKIN	IRON POT
TUMERIC	BRIGHT YELLOW	EGGS	POWDERED ROOT	NONE
BLOODROOT	RED ORANGE	WOOL YARN BODY PAINT	ROOT	ALUM
WILD GRAPE	PALE PURPLE	WOOL YARN	FRUIT SKIN	NONE
COLTSFOOT	SOFT GREEN	WOOL YARN EGGS	LEAVES	ALUM
MILKWEED	PALE YELLOW	WOOL YARN	ENTIRE PLANT	ALUM
MADDER	PINK—RED	WOOL YARN EGGS	ROOT	ALUM
RED CABBAGE	BLUE-GRAY ON WOOL ROBINS EGG BLUE ON EGGS	WOOL YARN EGGS	OUTER LEAVES	ALUM ON WOOL
WOAD	PALE BLUE	WOOL YARN	YOUNG LEAVES	LYE
INDIGO	DEEP BLUE	WOOL YARN	COMMERCIAL BLOCK	SPECTRALITE
SUMACH	GRAY	WOOL YARN EGGS	RED BERRIES	NONE
COCHINEAL	PINK DEEP RED	WOOL YARN EGGS	(COMES FROM AN INSECT)	ANY ON WOOL NONE ON EGGS

* A substance needed to fix the color or make it permanent.

was used as a remedy for "Breakbone Fever" in the 1840s. Milkweed pods with their silken fluff, goldenrod, and wild grasses and grains gathered now will be dried in time to adorn the altar at the Autumnal Equinox.

As the aromatic herbs begin to fill the rafters in the dry heat of the attic, and the braids of onions and garlic fill the cool darkness of the root cellar, the golden grain and yellow corn ripen in the fields under the waning August Sun.

To the ancients this was the Barley Moon, a time to contemplate the eternalness of life. Just as we are descended from the first woman and the first man, who descended from the Gods, so is the grain of the bread that we eat descended from the first grain ever gathered. By ritually eating the Lammas bread we are participating in a chain of events that stretches back through time to the Gods themselves. And here before us in the ripening fields is the promise of the future.

Everywhere there is abundance—in the herb garden, the vegetable garden, the field, and the orchard. The pantry shelves are lined with glistening glass jars that are filled with colorful fruits and vegetables preserved for Winter days: quarts of red tomatoes, cucumbers in slices or spears, dark red beets with cloves and cinnamon sticks, the yellow of corn, the orange of carrots—a feast for the eyes as well as the palate. The house is filled with delightful aromas as pickling spices are added to crocks of brine and exotic chutneys simmer on the stove.

But the time of abundance is drawing to a close. The fireflies of June and July have given way to katydids, whose scratchy calls to one another fill the evening air of August with the promise of frost in six weeks.

September

September

The yellow school buses of September days disappear into the early morning mist and reappear in the afternoon sunlight to disgorge their cargoes of kids. The warm September afternoons are still shaded by the lush green foliage of trees, but fields and meadows are a yellow sea of goldenrod interrupted only by islands of purple asters. Monarch butterflies stop to sip nectar as they begin their long migration to an isolated hilltop forest in Mexico, and wooly bear caterpillars migrate, too, to a place where they will hibernate for the Winter. The amount of black on their bodies does not foretell the severity of the Winter, but their presence foretells its coming.

Most of the harvests have been taken in and the clusters of grapes hang dark and heavy on the vine. The abundance of August has dwindled, but every few days there are tomatoes to pick. String beans were canned in quantity earlier in the season. Any that are picked now are strung on heavy white thread to hang in the attic. They will dry crisp and white like bony fingers of a skeletal hand, and when dropped into a pot of homemade soup, these leather breeches, as they are called, become plump and green again.

The hackberry tree in the corner of the orchard is the first to lose its leaves, which fall in swirling showers. These trees are hosts to lovely little black and brown butterflies speckled with white. They are also subject to a bacterial disease that causes strange tubercles to grow on the leaves, and some of the branches to grow what are called Witch Brooms. These Witch Brooms are bushy growths of twigs at the ends of some branches that really look like the classic besoms of the Halloween Crone. Most people consider them of slight interest or an ugly deformity, but a Pagan might consider them an amulet of good fortune and a special sign of blessing, like finding a four-leaf clover. Smaller Witch Brooms can be cut and kept in the house as amulets. Larger ones can be used as actual besoms to symbolically sweep the magic Circle clean.

The Beginning of the Wine Harvest

Sometime early in the month, as the sugar content of the plump black clusters reaches its peak, it is time to begin the grape harvest. It is traditional to begin this harvest by pouring a libation of red wine in the vineyard, saying something such as:

> *O Lord Dionysus*
> *God of wine and of resurrection*
> *Through whom we receive*
> *The spark of Spirit that animates us*
> *In your honor do we pour this libation*
> *We thank you Great God of the Vine*
> *For the harvest we are about to gather.*

Then the harvest baskets are slid along the ground under the vines as the juicy bunches of grapes are cut and dropped into them. Filled baskets are emptied into the hoppers, where the grapes are crushed. This crush goes into large open barrels, where primary fermentation takes place. Primary fermentation is possible because of the yeast, that grayish haze on the skin of grapes that converts sugar into alcohol. This process was so mysterious to ancient man, and the end product—like other natural substances able to induce an altered state of consciousness—so sacred, that every step was accompanied with ritual. Professional musicians performed as the grapes were picked, and they accompanied harvesters as they danced slowly in circles, crushing the grapes with their feet. The warmth of their bodies warmed the juice to a temperature that brought the yeast to life. Afterward, children were immersed in the blood-red liquid as a protection against illness.

When the primary fermentation on the skins is complete, the wine is pressed and the liquid is put into oak barrels, where it will undergo a secondary fermentation. This process, which converts alcoholic grape juice into fine and noble wine, is so like the spiritual transformation that takes place during all of life's initiations that this is a perfect time to perform a ritual designed to bring about increased spiritual awareness.

Arrange an altar in a wine cellar, if possible, with a purple altar cloth. Use an image of Bacchus or Dionysus and light two purple candles. Burn frankincense and adorn the altar with grape vine and bunches of grapes. Cast a Circle in your tradition and anoint yourself with red wine, tracing a pentacle on your forehead with the liquid. Then invoke the God with words such as:

> *O Lord Dionysus*
> *We invoke thee*
> *That we may know thee and love thee*
> *Like the wine that undergoes change in the barrel*
> *We will be transformed in Spirit*
> *By the light of thy love.*

Then sip some of the wine and gaze into one of the candle flames. Allow the wine and the candlelight to weave their spell, and feel the presence of the God.

The finished product of the vine was once so sacred that in the Rhine Valley of Germany, for example, wine was put into special stoneware jugs that were stamped with the visage of the God Himself. These jugs are called bellarmines, and the name, like the word *Beltane,* is probably derived from the Phoenician name *Baal,* which means Lord. Bellarmines came to be used to store a variety of liquids in the belief that the face of the god stamped on the neck of the jug would protect the contents from spoiling.

Since wine was, and is, such a sacred fluid, the Pagans of old naturally named this lunar month the Wine Moon. As you celebrate the night of the Full Wine Moon and dance the magical round in the moonlit Circle, pour some white wine in a silver cup. Before the rite is ended, if possible, catch Her reflection in the liquid, then take a sip. As the Moon-blessed wine casts its inner glow, sit quietly and feel your own spirit, of which the wine is a symbol. As the body is stilled and the spirit soars, feel on this night of magic a sense of the kind of transformation that takes place during true spiritual initiation.

Today the term Harvest Moon is applied to the Full Moon nearest to the Autumnal Equinox. This is because, it is said, in other times when harvesting was done by hand, as the days grew shorter farmers were able to work into the night in the brightness of Her light.

Throughout the month there are gourds and squash to harvest. The great variety and stunning patterns and colors of these fruits make them naturally decorative, and they can be used by the basketful to adorn porch, mantle, and dinner tables. The fact that they are born in the ninth month of the solar year also makes them sacred to the Goddess in Her aspect as the Earth Mother, and this makes them appropriate decorations for the altar and Circle at the Autumnal Equinox.

There are some gourds, too, that can be useful. The coyote melon, a gourd that grows in the American Southwest, is a small, round yellow to white gourd longitudinally banded with green. It dries out easily without rotting, and when it is completely dry the seeds inside make it a natural rattle, a perfect instrument for shamanistic rituals.

The gourds called dipper gourds have round or egg-shaped bases and long, thin necks that are sometimes crooked. They are bright yellow or orange with dark green at the base and stem. They can be made into useful dippers by taking a vertical slice off one side of the bulbous base and removing the seeds and stringy flesh, then hanging the gourd up to dry. In

A hackberry tree with Witch Brooms

An altar to Dionysus. A 2,000-year-old head of Dionysus from Italy hangs above the altar for a ritual following the pressing of the wine.

this case, though, it is wise to cut and clean several gourds to insure that at least one or two will dry nicely without deteriorating. Once dry, the gourd that loses its color and pattern can be engraved with magical signs if you like and shellacked to seal and preserve it. Such dippers have been used by shamans and brujos of the Southwest and Mexico for pouring or scattering magical brews and all sorts of ritual purposes. The large green "bird house" gourds lend themselves to similar uses.

At this time of year there are many varieties of ornamental corn available—either homegrown or sold at roadside stands. It is almost impossible to go for a ride through the countryside without coming back with a bunch of corn or a couple of gourds as souvenirs. There are golden corn, Indian corn, raspberry corn, and squaw corn. There are also bunches of ripe golden wheat. This is the time to select the ears of corn or a bundle of grain that will represent the Goddess in Her aspect as Bride for the ritual called Bride's Bed, which is performed at Imbolc in February. The bunch of corn or other grain should be brought into the house with ritual and honor as part of the Autumnal Equinox celebration. As you bring in the bunch of corn or grain and arrange it in a place of honor where it can remain until Imbolc, chant words such as:

> *Welcome Corn Mother*
> *We welcome Thee*
> *Welcome Corn Mother*
> *Blessed Be!*

As Lammas was the celebration of the first harvest, the Autumnal Equinox marks the time of the waning Sun, when food is harvested and stored for the coming of Winter, and seeds and grain are gathered for future generations of crops.

The gathering of seeds is a magical act and should begin with few deep breaths and a clear visualization of the idea that the life contained in the seeds will blossom and bear fruit in the coming year. Then as you approach each plant, on the day of the Full Moon, cast a Circle with your athame around the plant so that the transfer of power from the dying plant to the seed will be contained. As you collect the dried ears of corn, the pods of peas and beans, the squash and gourds, and the dried heads of marigolds and zinnias, whisper words such as:

> *From this Life*
> *Life to come.*

Later, remove the seeds from pods, ears, and seed heads. Seeds of fleshy fruits like squash should be rinsed and dried. Place the different types of seeds in small paper bags labeled and dated, and keep them in a cool, dry place where they will remain for six months, the entire dark half of the year, until being blessed at the Vernal Equinox.

As the nights of September are likely to be touched by frost, it is wise at this time to bring in the tender perennial herbs such as rosemary, verbena, or the scented geraniums that would be damaged by the frost. For indoor gardeners, or anyone who has the facilities indoors, this is a good time to plant basil or dill for an indoor garden to provide fresh herbs all Winter. One herb that loses its potency when dried is the purifying and protective rue, but volunteer seedlings can be dug up and potted now in case the fresh herb is needed one Winter's day.

As the waning light and cooler nights of September bring the growing season to a close, many herbs begin to wither or die back. So this is the time to gather those herbs of which the roots are the parts used. A general rule is that if the aerial parts of a plant are to be used, those parts should be gathered as the plant is coming into bloom, when the magical power in the aerial parts is greatest. If the root is the part of the herb to be used, it should be collected when the plant has died back and the magical power has returned to the root.

Of all the herbs used for magical purposes, those of which the root are used are among the most famous (or infamous). Every part of the herb aconite, or monkshood, is deadly poisonous, but the root or rhizomes are the most potent part of all. Aconite does have some medicinal properties, but the plant is so poisonous that collecting it can be dangerous. It was one of the prime ingredients in Witches' flying ointments.

Another herb used in these flying ointments was belladonna. So poisonous is this plant that the name of the genus, *atropa*, comes from Atropos, the name of one of the Three Fates. Atropos is the one that cuts the thread of life at death.

One of the most famous of all roots is mandrake, or mandragora. At one time it was considered so magical that many legends grew up around it. The most popular of these legends states that when the plant was pulled out of the ground it uttered such a horrible scream that the herbalist gathering it was driven mad. One safe way to collect the herb was to tie a hungry dog to the plant and leave some food a few feet away. The dog, of course, would pull out the mandrake root while trying to reach the food. The roots of mandrake sometimes grow doubled or tripled, and with a little imagination these roots can be seen to resemble male or female human figures. These roots can be carried as amulets. The ones that resemble a female figure are carried by women who wish to conceive. Those that resemble a male figure are carried by men who want to retain or regain their virility. Since mandrake roots that resemble human figures are rare, a little carving to help the shape will increase the magical power of the root and in fact make it an excellent amulet of fertility or virility. Mandrake root carved or uncarved is an excellent amulet for protection as well.

Angelica is another herb whose root is used rather than its aerial parts. The root is used as an amulet of protection and purification. It is also used as an incense to dispel any evil that is psychic in origin. It can be worn in a small pouch or hung up in the house.

Elcampane is a tall plant that grows wild in much of the country and blooms in late Summer. When it begins to die back its roots can be gathered and quickly dried (in a low oven about 150° with the door open a crack). Larger roots can be cut in half. These roots can be used for love charms and amulets.

Valerian is a natural sedative, and its roots are the most potent part of the plant. Because of its sedative properties it can be used in charms to end or prevent arguments. It is also useful in bath preparations for purification and relaxation prior to performing any ritual.

The root of yellow dock, dried and ground to a powder, can be steeped in boiling water and the infusion used to anoint the doors of your office, home, or studio so that good fortune will enter.

As the days of September pass and the trees become tinged with the colors that will dominate the landscape a month hence, we begin to notice everywhere that the porches and doorways of many homes are being adorned with the fruits of the season. Bunches of colorful Indian corn hang on painted front doors and cornstalks adorn lampposts. Baskets of gourds and varieties of squash decorate steps, stoops, and porches. As we hang a bunch of corn by our own front door, it is a sign that this is a Pagan home where the ancient Gods are welcomed and venerated. This is not the case, of course, with everyone who hangs a bunch of corn on their door or parks a pumpkin on their porch, but it is a sign that more and more people every year are responding to an inner urge to celebrate the cycle of the seasons by gathering the fruits of the season.

As the evening skies of September flush with pink, the calls of wild geese are heard. Their silhouettes appear overhead and stir within us something ancient and winged. This is only a practice flight for the long migration that lies ahead, but it is a sign that the days of Summer are drawing to an end.

October

October

The misty mornings of October melt into golden afternoons and crystal moonlit nights. Everywhere there is color. The maple trees that surround our house envelope it in a cloak of buttery yellow and carpet the ground, while the cadmium orange sumach crowns the hill above the vineyard, all in contrast to the still-green grass and clear blue skies. Corn that has been left in the field to dry for Winter feed has been bleached bone white, and it rattles like dancing skeletons in the October breezes.

Inside, the first fires have been kindled in the big kitchen fireplace to ward off the Winter chill. There is the faint aroma of camphor wafting through the house from the familiar patterns of the patchwork quilts that have been brought out of storage to warm the frosty nights.

The last of the herbs have been gathered, and they hang from the smoky beams of the kitchen ceiling. There are the culinary thymes, savory, aromatic sage, the medicinal mints, coltsfoot, and southernwood, and magical mugwort, wormwood, and artemisia bathed in its own moonlight. All hang in the flickering light of the hearth fire, drying in its warm glow.

This is the time of the apple harvest: winesaps, greenings, macintosh, red and yellow delicious, and the antique varieties of sops of wine, sheep nose and smokehouse. There are apples to fill fruit bowls for immediate eating, apples that keep well for Winter storage, and apples that make the best pie ever. The back porch smells of baskets of apples in the afternoon Sun, and the house smells of hot applesauce laced with cinnamon, which is canned by the case.

Apples have always been magically important. The Celts "wassailed" their apple trees to insure a bountiful harvest in the coming year. Traditionally wassail was made of hard cider that was heated with spices and had apples floating on top. These apples, when heated enough, would burst their skins, and the white flesh would form a froth on top of the wassail. There is as much reason to believe that wassailing was performed at Samhain or Halloween as it was at Yule. Halloween is the time of the apple harvest,

The Night when the Other World Is Very Near

and there are many Halloween traditions in which apples are very important. Halloween was the New Year of the Celtic calendar, and probably several New Year traditions got shifted to Yuletide when the calendar was changed. Wassailing the apple trees, no doubt, was one of these.

Candy apples are a traditional trick or treat gift at Halloween. Another Halloween tradition is bobbing for apples, or "dooking," as it is called in Scotland. In this game apples are floated in a tub of water and players try to take apples out with their teeth and are not allowed to use their hands. This game may have developed directly from the apples that floated on the wassail of earlier Halloweens.

Another traditional Halloween game is apple on a string. Similar to bobbing for apples, the object of this game is for a player to get hold of the suspended apple with his or her mouth without using his or her hands. This game may have evolved from people playing a similar game while the apples still hung on the tree, and this may have been done in imitation of certain animals. But it is more likely that these games developed in the spirit of fun and play that is the essence of Pagan celebration.

Apples also have a history of being used for healing ("An apple a day keeps the doctor away"), especially for curing warts. The most typical method is to slice an apple in half and rub both halves over the wart or affliction to be cured. Then put the two halves of the apple back together and bury them in the Earth while reciting an enchantment to the effect that as the apple wastes away, so will the wart or other affliction.

When an apple is sliced in half horizontally it reveals hidden within its core a five-pointed star. When an apple is being cut in half for magical purposes it should be cut this way in order to take full advantage of the secret magical sign. And of course it should be cut with the magically charged white-handled knife.

The apple harvest can be celebrated on the day that it is completed with a meal that features apples, apple fritters, apple pie, or applesauce. Select one tree to represent all of the apple trees in the orchard, whether it is the oldest, tallest, or most productive. Draw and consecrate a Circle around the tree and stand within it facing the tree. Holding a cup of spiced cider or apple wine, anoint the tree by drawing a pentacle with a finger dipped in the cup of liquid. Draw the pentacle at eye level on the tree trunk or just below where all the branches begin. Recite something such as:

> Here's to thee Apple tree
> Flowers at Beltane
> Fruit at Samhain
> Apple tree, Blessed be!

Then drink a toast to the tree and pour a libation at its roots, and eat the food of the feast within the Circle.

The final harvest of the year is the hazelnut harvest. The nuts, which are borne in clusters of woody, flowerlike hulls, are gathered in loosely woven baskets toward the end of the month. They will be left in the hulls in the wickerwork baskets to cure on the kitchen hearth for a few weeks, being turned frequently to prevent them from becoming moldy. By Halloween some of the nuts will have dried enough to loosen from the hulls. These will be picked out and can be eaten, along with apples at the Samhain ritual. They can also be served to friends on Halloween night, and some of the nuts still in the hulls are a beautiful decoration for the Samhain altar and the Halloween trick or treat table.

The hazel tree has long been sacred to the Celts and is symbolic of wisdom, secret knowledge, and divination. The legendary Nine Hazels that surrounded Connlas Well in Ireland bore flowers and fruit at the same time. Forked hazel rods have long been used for dowsing sources of underground water or minerals, and hazel wood is a traditional wood for magical wands. The wands of the Druids were of hazel. Its power is such that the staffs of the Celtic Christian bishops were of hazel.

Although hazelnuts are gathered in late Autumn, according to Robert Graves, the tree's month in the Celtic Tree Calendar is from August 5 to September 1, the nutting (castrating) season, which symbolically associates it with several gods of death and resurrection.

The most obvious of these gods is Attis, the Phrygian God whose mother conceived him (according to one version of the myth) by placing an almond on her lap, which then disappeared. Attis was so beautiful a young man that Cybele, the Great Mother, creator of Gods and humans, fell in love with him. He was caused to marry another, but Cybele had such a fit of jealous rage that Attis went mad. He castrated himself under a pine tree and violets sprang from the drops of his blood. Before dying, he presented his severed organs to Cybele, who kept them carefully wrapped, and with the aid of Zeus, Attis arose from the dead every Spring.

The cult of Cybele and Attis, with its eunuch priests, spread from Phrygian Turkey to Greece and then to Rome. It bears a strong resemblance to the Babylonian myth of Adonis, and even has some associations with the Egyptian Isis and Osiris. And its theme is repeated once again in the Germanic and Teutonic cults of Ing and Nerthus. Ing was a priest of Nerthus, the Earth Mother who consumes her consort to revitalize herself after she has depleted herself by the outpouring of her life-giving energy in the Spring. Ing is the priest that accompanies the wagon or cart of Nerthus as it is drawn about the countryside for the fertility rites of Spring. It is he alone who knows when she is present. Ing sacrificed himself to the Goddess by castration, but was born again after a period of gestation, through the Earth Mother, thereby becoming a God.

The association of the hazel with the season of castration, and also with things hidden in the Earth, links it also to the universal magic of the cycle of birth, death, and rebirth, especially at the Halloween season when the veil between the worlds is very thin. And so, at this time of the year make a string of nine hazelnuts (nine being the number of the month of the hazel in the Celtic Tree Calendar) and tie the ends of the string together to form a circle. Consecrate it in the smoke of the Samhain Fire, chanting:

> *Hazelnuts nine in a ring*
> *By the smoke of the Samhain Fire bring*
> *Protection to this house and those within*
> *Blessed be this charm of nuts and string.*

Then hang it in the house as an amulet of protection for the coming year. Eating hazelnuts at the Samhain Sabbat is a symbolic way of partaking of the God. Always put a handful of nuts aside to bury during the Spring rites in order to attune yourself with the rhythms of the eternal cycle of birth, death, and rebirth.

The sights and sounds and smells of October bring about in all of us subtle changes, and as our bodies begin to change metabolism, preparing us for shorter Winter days, our consciousness begins to shift from the more actively mental to the more psychically receptive state appropriate to the dark half of the year. As all of these changes are taking place we are busy preparing for the most magical night of the year, Halloween. (We still use the name Halloween interchangeably with Samhain, as it still has the magical impact that it once did when we were children, and the utterance of the word stirred in us the excitement of dimly remembered Sabbats of other lives almost forgotten.)

The outward manifestations of these internal changes begin to appear all around the house. On the back porch a pumpkin and gourds are the centerpiece on the picnic table, while the grapevine wreath on the door is adorned with a huge black bow dotted with orange Witches flying across white moons. The Witches on the bow match almost exactly Hecate, our flying Witch weathervane and protective mascot that straddles her broomstick in an eternal flight path over our smokehouse. On the front porch pumpkins and colorful squash nestle against an old red butter churn, and sprays of bittersweet are added to the bunch of Indian corn that hangs by the front door. Bundles of dried cornstalks flank the front steps, and as the month progresses grinning jack-o'-lanterns stare from the windows. We carefully cut the eyeholes of each jack-o'-lantern so that they appear to be watching anyone that approaches the front porch. As night falls their flaming grins and fiery eyes stare from every window.

The origin of the jack-o'-lantern is obscure, but no doubt started in the New World. The name used to apply to a natural phenomenon, a luminous glow in the eastern sky after sunset. It may be that since the sunset in the west symbolized death, this glow in the east symbolized the spiritual survival of death.

Today in Ireland, candles are lit in cottage windows on Samhain night to welcome the spirits of the deceased. In faraway Japan, on a night equivalent to Halloween, the spirits of the deceased are welcomed home by glowing paper lanterns hung by garden gates. How the candle got inside the pumpkin may forever remain a mystery, but there can be little doubt that the jack-o'-lantern originated as a beacon light to welcome the spirits who roam freely among us on this night of Halloween.

As the night of the Great Sabbat draws closer, the work of preparation intensifies. There are cookies to bake—orange ones in the shape of pumpkin heads and chocolate ones shaped like cats—then the lollipops to make, in clear orange, flavored to match, or golden amber flavored butterscotch. They are poured into molds shaped like Witches on broomsticks, cats, owls, hens on nests, roosters, and turkeys. On Halloween morning we make about two and a half dozen of the traditional candy apples using our own winesaps that were specifically chosen for their size and redness.

The wonderful tradition of Halloween trick or treat raises a very interesting question for anyone who wishes to celebrate a truly religious Sabbat. It has been said that it is better to celebrate Sabbat rites later than earlier because of the ebb and flow of psychic currents. We prefer to perform our rites of Samhain as these psychic currents are waxing, because as anyone who has felt "Christmas spirit" knows, it is strongest on Christmas Eve, and the day after Christmas is a big letdown. And so we perform the solemn rites of Samhain near midnight the night before Halloween.

Samhain marks the transition from the light half of the year to the dark. Now is the time that the Lady, the fruitful Mother, has been delivered of her child, the fruits of the Earth. The harvest has been completed. She steps aside as the Horned One steps forward. Now is the time that our focus shifts from the physical side of life to the spiritual, for at this time of transition the veil is very thin between the two worlds.

At this time of year the abundance of fruit and vegetables begins to slow. It is a time when our ancient ancestors gathered what they could store and then supplemented their Winter diets either by hunting wild animals or by slaughtering domestic ones. So this lunar month is called the Blood Moon. As you cast the Esbat Circle on this moonlit Autumn night and fill the cup with blood-red wine, know that you will be joined in the sacred dance not only by the unseen presence of departed friends and family so close at this time of year, but also by the spirits of animals as well, perhaps of those that have died so that we may have food. In this age of assembly line slaughterhouses and meatpacking plants, it is especially appropriate that on this night of the Blood Moon we who are on the Pagan path ritually ask the understanding of our animal sisters and brothers, bless them, and bid them merry meet, merry part, and merry meet again.

Samhain is a celebration of death, and as such it is marked by several traditions. One of these is the Feast of the Dead, or the Dumb Supper as it is sometimes called. This has many variations—from a complete meal shared by the living, with places set at the table for the dead, to the simple leaving of cakes and wine, or any similar combination, by the fireside on Samhain Night. And this is the most traditional time for communication with the dead. For this reason, after welcoming them into our Samhain Circle through the Western Gate, the direction of death, you can allow the spirits of the deceased to communicate with you if they so desire. One method is the wineglass.

Similar to the ouija board but without the undeserved sinister reputation, the wineglass is just that, an inverted wineglass (the champagne type is better than the white wine type, as it is less likely to tip). The glass is surrounded by a circle of letters. An alphabet in Gothic style drawn on squares of white paper help to create an appropriate atmosphere.

It must be mentioned here that may occultists turn up their highly evolved noses at such devices as the ouija board, the pendulum board, and, no doubt, the wineglass, preferring instead personal mediumship, or channeling, as it is currently being called. But we believe that entities willing to take control of the body or voice of another individual cannot be of the highest caliber. Nor is every scene that passes before the inner eye psychic or spiritual, or the motivations that created them always spiritually pure. This is not to say that we do not believe in either channeled information or that which is received psychically. We most certainly do, but we have seen many instances of self-delusion, which is one of the greatest barriers to true spiritual development.

The wineglass, on the other hand, has several built-in safety devices. It cannot easily be operated alone, so spiritual possession is less likely, and since two or more people are operating it, self-delusion is not so easy. It is interesting to note, too, that the wineglass brings with it some intrinsic symbolism. It is a vessel or container for wine, itself a symbol for spiritual awareness, so the wineglass is a container for spiritual knowledge.

The wineglass can be used within the Samhain Circle. The four quarters of the Circle may be marked with candles in jack-o'-lanterns, and an extra candle, an indigo blue one (the color symbolizing the higher spiritual planes), should also be lit. This candle might be anointed with oil and marked with a rune such as $\int$ that describes the travel between the planes. After a moment of meditation each person present places a fingertip on the upturned base of the wineglass and the traditional "Is anyone here that wishes to give us a message?" is asked. Then as the glass slides from one letter to the next, rapidly spelling out messages, read the words. You may find it easier to use a tape recorder because it can get confusing. At this, the most solemn of Pagan festivals, the messages are often personal and profound.

Once the more solemn of the rites of Samhain have been performed, we arrange all the treats on our old pine dinner table. A centerpiece of jack-o'-lanterns and gourds are surrounded by trays of cookies, dishes of lollipops, and platters of gleaming candy apples, and a cauldron of popcorn and a spider (a three-legged frying pan) full of candy corn all await the trick-or-treaters.

The sounds of small feet shuffling up our path through the dry leaves of October announce the arrival of the trick-or-treaters long before their knocks at the door. This one night of the year it has become a tradition for us to have an open house for our neighbors. Many of the parents escort their children for trick or treat. This gives us an opportunity to visit with neighbors that we normally wouldn't see from one end of the year to the next. As the children gaze wide-eyed at the array of Halloween treats placed before them and slowly fill their bags with one of each, their parents are met with cups of spiced mulled wine to offset the chill of the night air and to protect them from evil spirits.

Among the Halloween costumes—the Nixons, the Rambos, the ballerinas, and the clowns—there are others of more ancient design. There is the inevitable Witch, really the Goddess herself, in her aspect as the Crone, her tall, pointed hat actually a form of dunce cap that uses "pyramid power." The Witch, or Crone, drew power through the pointed top and sent it out to do her bidding via the flared brim. Her black dress reminds us that the Goddess has her dark (but not evil) side too, and her broomstick is her shaman's horse upon which she rides over the Moon to other planes and realms. There are ghosts draped in parental linen and skeletons with glow-in-the-dark bones, reminding us that on this night of the year the veil that separates the living from the dead is very thin.

But possibly the most interesting costumes of all is the one that took the least effort. There are always at least a handful of children that just put on old clothes and blacken their faces with burnt cork. Some of them might take the initiative to tie a bundle to the end of a stick and call themselves hobos. (The Fool of the Tarot deck about to begin a journey of initiations?) Others might carry a broom or a brush and call themselves chimney sweeps. This raises some very interesting points about this costume and Halloween. It is lucky, especially for a bride, to shake hands with a "sweep," and this may be because a sweep goes up the chimney with his brush, like the Crone goes up the chimney with her broomstick, or as the shaman goes up the smokehole of his yurt or tent on the tree trunk that is sometimes called his horse. Or it may be that the sooty appearance of the sweep recalls that ancient tribe of people that came to be known as Faeries, who lived in turf-covered mound houses and who may have entered and left those houses by way of the smokehole—either in the flesh or in spirit.

But whether he is called a male witch, a shaman, or a Faerie, the Man in Black is the priest of the coven according to testimony extracted at the Witch trials in Europe. One reason the priest of the coven and other members, for that matter, rubbed themselves with soot was no doubt in order to camouflage themselves on the way to and from secret meetings held at night during the period of persecution known as the Burning Times.

Another reason is that one of the prime ingredients in all flying ointments is soot. Other ingedients are hellebore, hemlock, henbane, aconite, and amonita. All of these herbs are extremely poisonous and no doubt when applied externally could induce altered states of consciousness that could enable the priest or shaman to make contact with the spirit world or even the Gods themselves. It is possible that when applied externally these herbs were far less dangerous than if they had been ingested, but no actual formulas still exist to our knowledge, and experimentation would be far too dangerous. Whether the soot was an active ingredient or merely provided a disguise is a matter of conjecture. Or it could be that by wearing soot the Man in Black was performing the same act of Fire magic that our ancestors did when they covered themselves with the ashes of the Need Fire, that ancient forerunner of the Sabbat Fire.

As we watch the children leave the light of our front porch and disappear into the darkness on their way to the next farmhouse up the road, we wonder if they can possibly comprehend the age and importance of the traditions they are helping to preserve.

The earliest representation of a man wearing a costume dates from the paleolithic period; it is a painting in the Cave des Trois Freres in Ariage, France. This painting of a man wearing the skin of an animal with the antlers of a stag is surrounded by depictions of animals that are easily visible; but The Sorcerer, as this painting is called, is hidden in a crevice high up in the chamber called the Sanctuary, and it can be properly seen only after a steep climb through a narrow and twisting passage.

There are figures from early Bronze Age sites at Mohenjo-Daro in the Indus Valley that are depicted as wearing not only the horns or mask of a

The wineglass—spirit communication in the Samhain Circle

The table set for Halloween trick or treat

bull but the skin as well.

The Pharaohs of Egypt performed a sacred dance wearing a bull's tail at the Sed Heb or Tail festival at the temple of Min. When the priests of ancient Egypt wished to invoke their gods they wore masks over their entire heads. Many tomb and temple paintings depict priests wearing the mask of the jackel-headed god Anubis. Masked priests can be distinguished from paintings of the gods themselves by noticing the artist's device of portraying the masked priest as having the lappets of the wig over both shoulders. If a god is being portrayed, only the lappet over the nearest shoulder is painted.

When the king and high priest of Mesopotamia invoked the God Ashur, or when the queen and high priestess became the Goddess Ishtar, they wore appropriate headdresses. When the Hopi Indian puts on a Kachina mask, he loses his own identity and becomes the spirit portrayed by the mask.

Theodore of Tarsus was archbishop of Canterbury from 668 to 690. He condemned "anyone who goes about as a stag or a bull, that is, making himself into a wild animal, and putting on the heads of beasts, those who in such wise transform themselves into the appearance of a wild beast, penance for three years." There can be little doubt that the Cretan Bull— half man, half bull, which awaited its victims at the heart of the Labyrinth— was a priest wearing the head and skin of a bull.

Masks, too, have long been associated with death. The gold death masks discovered by Schliemann at Mycenae covering the faces of the corpses of heroes or noblemen were complete with beards and eyelashes. No doubt they were intended to preserve the likenesses of the deceased throughout the ages. That was certainly the purpose of the most famous death mask of all, the gold and lapis portrait of the "boy king" Tutankhamen.

Many of the tribes of the Indians of North America buried their dead with death masks made of wood, while those of South and Central America covered the faces of their deceased with masks of jade or torquoise mosaic. The ceremonial masks used by the Indians of the Pacific Northwest, on the other hand, do not represent the spirits of the deceased but, like the Kachina masks of the Hopi of the Southwest, they represent Nature spirits. Through their rituals they invoke these spirits by ceremonial dances, or by recreating their myths in order to appease them, because in the words of one Eskimo shaman, "All of the creatures we have to kill to eat, all those we have to strike down and destroy to make clothes for ourselves, have souls, as we have."

According to testimony extracted from Witches during the trials of the persecution, the Man in Black often led the magical dance disguised as a dog, goat, bull, deer, or black cat in Germany, France, and England. The most recent example of such ritual costuming is the Ooser of Dorset, a painted wooden mask with a human face and bull's horns. It is unfortunate that this treasured Pagan relic had to be stolen during the first quarter of this century.

Whether masks represent the Gods themselves, Nature or animal spirits, or the spirits of the dead, they have become firmly attached to the traditions of Samhain and the time of the year when the spirit world is very close, when we are filled with the wonder and mystery of other realms.

For this reason, and because during the persecution masks were worn to protect the identity of Pagan worshippers, you might want to make masking a part of your Samhain Sabbat. Masks can be made to represent the God and Goddess, and can be worn by priest and priestess when the Gods are invoked. Or masks might be made to represent the three aspects of the Goddess—the Maid, the Mother, and the Crone—so that the priestess can choose one should the Goddess speak through her. Or likewise, the priest might choose a mask that represents the God in his aspect of death or of rebirth, should the God wish to speak through him. Masks can also be made to represent the spirits of Nature. They can be made of an endless variety of materials and decorated with even more. They don't even have to be worn but just hung at various points about the perimeter of the Samhain Circle, where they can become animated by the flickering lights of the candles one moment and disappear into the shadows the next. Or a mask can be passed around the Circle to be tried on by any member of the group. It is amazing how the donning of a mask can get the psychic juices flowing. But whether they are worn or not, masks serve as reminders that we are always surrounded by the realms of the spirits and the Gods themselves, and on this night more than any other, they are very close.

Along with masking, costuming, and communicating with the spirit world, Halloween is a traditional time for divining the future. One reason for this is that for the ancient Celts, Samhain was the beginning of the new year, and what better time than the first of the year to learn what the future holds for us. It is a part of this tradition that the divination be done with the fruits of the season.

Hazelnuts, especially, are associated with divination, as the forked branch of hazel is the traditional "divining rod." Young girls would divine the name of their future husbands by naming one hazelnut for each boy they knew, then roasting them all by an open fire. The name of the first nut to jump would be the name of the first boy she would marry. This method of divination can easily be applied to any question that has multiple answers, or even one that requires a simple yes or no.

Apples, too, were used for divination as well as for several Halloween games. One method for a girl to learn the identity of her future partner was to cut an apple into nine equal parts, eat eight of them, and then toss the ninth one over the left shoulder and turn around quickly. She would then catch a glimpse of the face of her husband-to-be. This method might apply just as well to other future events or even to former lives.

For anyone who is not interested in, or already knows, the identity of their mate or partner, Halloween is still a perfect time for the laying out of Tarot cards or the casting of runes. You might want to cast your own runes within the Samhain Circle, and keep a deck of Tarot cards or the runes handy for anyone who might want their fortunes told on this night.

Trick or treat itself seems to have originated in Europe as a Beltane or May Day tradition. In England, children carrying miniature Maypoles and a doll called Lady of the May begged for pennies door to door, while in Alsace, France, groups of children with a doll called Little May Rose, who was dressed as a bride, went from door to door asking for gifts and threatening the loss of fowls, grapes on the vine, nuts on the tree, and corn in the fields to anyone who did not contribute.

As the hours of trick or treat draw to a close and the platters of cookies and candy apples are emptied, a small group of friends begin to gather. It has become a tradition for us to gather around the table to snack on the fruits of the season and to taste the recently bottled champagnes while their children all sit in front of our TV set and watch videotapes of "The Addams Family," "The Legend of Sleepy Hollow," and "It's the Great Pumpkin, Charlie Brown." Eventually the sleepy children, filled with candy and exhausted from hours of trick or treating, are carried home to be put to bed to dream dreams of goblins and popcorn, Witches and candy apples.

At last Dan and I are left alone by our kitchen fire to contemplate the magic of this night. As the "Witching hour" of midnight approaches, we gaze into the flames and imagine other times, in other places, when on this night Samhain Fires glowed on every hilltop, and hearts were united in the joy of the season. As Moonset darkens this haunted night and the spirits gather at the doors and windows, we stare into the fire and the wind howls down the chimney as the Crone flies overhead. When the dying fire has been banked and the candles in the jack-o'-lanterns have been extinguished, we leave a plate of cakes and a cup of wine for whatever spirits seek the comfort of our kitchen hearth tonight, and we climb the stairs to sleep and to dream of Sabbat rites and Samhain Fires still to come.

November

November

The golden leaves that were the glory of October now lie dead and brown on the frosty ground, and bare black branches etch their silhouettes against the bleak gray sky. In contrast to the coldness outside, homes are warm inside with fireglow, and the nights that begin so early now twinkle with candlelight. This is the time of year for psychic, as opposed to physical, activity, and the time for candle magic and fire magic.

In some traditions, such as the Celtic, the household hearth fire was extinguished and a new fire for the year was kindled at Samhain, no doubt from the community Samhain Fire itself. When kindling the first fires to warm the home and protect it against the Winter's cold, invoke the element of Fire, requesting that as the fire provides life-preserving warmth it also provides its protection from loss or injury by fire. This request should not only be ritually chanted into the flames but also written on wood pulp paper and cut into triangles to be consumed by the flames as well.

As the paper burns, chant something such as:

O Element of Fire
Give us the warmth and the light
Of your transforming flames
Yet harm us not with your
All-consuming power
In the name of the Goddess and the God
Blessed be this Fire.

Then as a sort of thank you in advance, feed the fire a sprig of pyracantha (firethorn), whose pointed thorns and flame-colored berries link it with the element of Fire.

At the close of the Samhain Sabbat the altar candles were extinguished, signifying both the dark half of the year and the dark half of life which is

Consecrating Candles for Magic and Ritual

death. At Yule, new altar candles will be lit signifying the rebirth of the solar year and the midpoint of the dark half of the year. This quiet month of November, between the excitement and preparation of Samhain and Yule, is a perfect time to anoint and prepare the new altar candles as well as candles for any other magical purposes for the coming year.

For anointing or dressing altar candles, use an altar oil, the main ingredients of which are olive oil and frankincense. Altar oil is also used to anoint other ritual tools and the altar itself. Rub a drop between your palms and apply it to the candle from the center upwards and from the center downwards, both at the same time, turning the candle so that the entire surface is coated lightly with the oil. (It is easiest to prepare candles in pairs.) When both candles have been dressed with oil, light them. Holding one in each hand, raise them high and consecrate them in the names of the God and Goddess, then snuff the flames and wrap the candles in a triangle of white linen until they are needed.

Oils used to anoint candles for other magical purposes vary greatly. There are healing oils made by soaking healing herbs in oils, then pressing the oil and adding fresh herbs. This process can be repeated many times until a very potent oil is pressed off. Another method of adding the healing or magical properties of herbs to oil is to obtain commercially produced essential oils of the herbs and add just a few drops to the oil.

To create a magnetic oil, place a natural magnet (magnetite crystal is unbelievably powerful) in a small vial of oil from New Moon to Full.

Mandrake root gives good, all-purpose magical properties to oil, but it should stand in the oil from the last quarter of the Moon to the first because the power of this root lies in its secret hidden nature, in keeping with the dark phase of the Moon. This is true of many herbs when the root is the part that is used.

Another root that will impart its magical properties to oil is High John the Conqueror root. The oil, Conqueror oil, can be applied to sports equipment as well as candles to give a magical advantage in competitive games. (We don't consider a magical advantage any less ethical than a physical or intellectual advantage as long as we "harm none.")

The most powerful candle magic comes from using the most appropriate oil with the most appropriately colored candle. There are two systems of thought for determining what color candle to use. One is the primary color system, which is based on the fact that all colors can be made from the three primary colors red, yellow, and blue, plus the two neutrals white and black. White represents pure light and black represents the absence of light. The three primary colors correspond to the three divisions of the planes of existence: red to the physical, yellow to the mental, and blue to the spiritual.

Certain traditions of ceremonial magic perceive "God" as being, consciousness, and bliss. These three attributes correspond to the physical, mental, and spiritual aspects of man and to the three primary colors. The secondary colors green, orange, and purple are made by combining any two primarys, and the tertiary colors yellow-green, red-orange, or blue-violet, etc. are made by combining a primary and a secondary color.

The primary, secondary, and tertiary colors all fit together to form the color wheel. In the tradition of color physics the color wheel always appears with yellow at the top, so beginning at the top and going clockwise, or deosil, the color wheel is yellow, yellow-green, green, blue-green, blue, blue-violet, violet, red-violet, red, red-orange, orange, yellow-orange, and back at the top, yellow.

If the color wheel is reversed, with yellow at the bottom and its opposite violet at the top, then there is an obvious connection to the magic Circle with its four cardinal points, and to the Wheel of the Year with its solstices and equinoxes. By dividing the magic Circle in half with a line from the eastern point, which symbolizes birth, to the western point, which symbolizes death, the northern half of the circle becomes the realm of spiritual existence, which corresponds both to the dark half of the Wheel of the Year divided through the Vernal and Autumnal Equinoxes and to the cool dark half of the color wheel divided through blue-green and red-orange. The southern half of the magic Circle corresponds to physical life through all its stages from birth to death, and to the warm light half of the Wheel of the Year and warm, bright colors of the lower half of the color wheel.

The second system of color is similar to the Doctrine of Signatures, which states that an herb will bear a sign indicating which organ it corresponds to or what disease it cures. Using this system, candle colors are chosen because of what they look like. Red looks like flesh and blood, so it is used for very physical purposes: the life force, vital energy, and sex. Green is the color of money and growing things, so green candles are used for rituals to increase wealth, etc.

Pink, which is red plus the white of pure white light, represents a spiritual form of love. While red represents physical sexual love, deep reds like rust or maroon are red plus black (the absence of spiritual light), and are used (usually negatively) for anger and conflict. They are the color of Mars, the God of War. Purple, which is a combination of the physical red and the spiritual blue, is one of the most spiritual colors in its light violet aspect combined with white. It corresponds both to the northernmost point of the magic Circle and to the darkest part of the Wheel of the Year—from Samhain to Yule. In its vibrant and intense form of deep purple it is the right color for ritual sex. By its very nature purple in its pure state is so

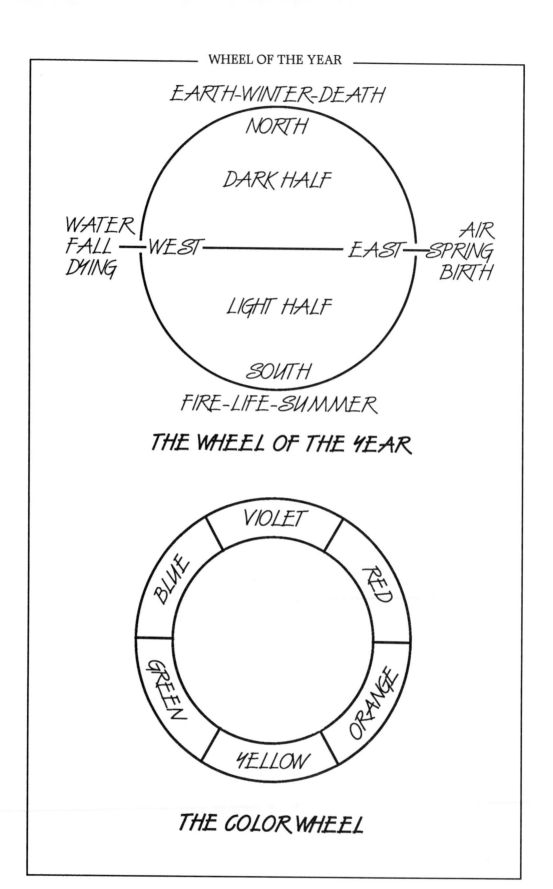

EARTH-WINTER-DEATH

NORTH

DARK HALF

WATER
FALL —— WEST ——————————— EAST —— AIR
DYING   SPRING
                                                        BIRTH

LIGHT HALF

SOUTH

FIRE-LIFE-SUMMER

THE WHEEL OF THE YEAR

VIOLET

BLUE

RED

GREEN

ORANGE

YELLOW

THE COLOR WHEEL

deep that it cannot easily be affected by black.

It is often helpful to use both the color wheel system and the corresponding color system (colors that look like what they are used for), or use one system to check the other.

The power of the color of the candle, and the oil with which it is dressed, can be further enhanced by inscribing the candle with a rune or runes. For example, a green candle dressed with magnetized oil and inscribed with the rune ᚠ is bound to attract financial rewards. A black candle inscribed with the rune ᚦ (sometimes called the destroyer of evil) and dressed with Conqueror oil is an excellent protection, especially against psychic attack.

The rune ᚷ means a uniting partnership and the dynamic energies that flow between the male/female polarities. If this rune is inscribed on a red candle dressed with musk oil (synthetic of course), it will insure a night of sexual fun and games. (Again, using magic to attract a partner is just as ethical as using hair color or cosmetics—in fact, far more so, because to work magic is to be honest, and it is an extension of your own personality, in the truest sense.)

If the rune ᚷ is inscribed on a pink candle dressed with rose oil, it can enhance the flow of psychic energy between good friends and enable them to pool their resources in acts of magic. The same rune inscribed on a deep purple candle dressed with altar oil can maximize the dynamic flow of creative energy generated during ritual sex magic.

Runes have corresponding numbers depending on their position in the rune row, and using these numbers increases the power of the inscribed rune. The number of ᚠ is one because it is the first rune in the row, so inscribing it once on a green candle is in keeping with its numerical value. Three is the value of ᚦ, so the rune can be inscribed three times on one candle, or once on each of three candles, or incorporated into a design such as ᚴ.

Astrological and planetary signs and abstract symbols can be used as well as runes, and these, too, have their corresponding numbers and colors. The sign for Aquarius, for example, ♒ inscribed eleven times on a candle of indigo or electric blue, is a powerful tool when used in conjunction with a chanted affirmation just before going to sleep, to bring about clairvoyant dreams or astral travel.

Whenever candles are being selected, purchased, or made for magical purposes, unless they are molded into a specific magical shape, the standard twelve-inch taper is traditional. There is one exception: Those spiral candles in silver, when consecrated to the Goddess of the Moon, can bring amazing results in Moon magic. Another variation of the shape is to carve a candle

RUNE	MEANING	PURPOSE	#	COLOR
ᚠ	MATERIAL WEALTH	PROSPERITY	1	GREEN
ᚢ	STRENGTH	FOR PERSONAL STRENGTH & COURAGE	2	GREEN or BROWN
ᚦ	PROTECTION FROM EVIL	PROTECTION— AS FROM EVIL MAGIC	3	BLACK
ᚨ	ODIN ANCESTOR	TO GAIN ANCIENT WISDOM	4	INDIGO or PURPLE
ᚱ	TRAVEL QUEST	TO FIND THAT WHICH YOU SEEK	5	BLUE or VIOLET
<	TRANSFORMING FIRE	AS AN OFFERING OR FOR SKILL IN A CRAFT	6	WHITE or GOLD
ᚷ	UNION	PARTNERSHIPS OR SEX MAGIC	7	PINK, RED OR PURPLE
ᚹ	JOY	FOR HAPPINESS OR HARMONY	8	PINK OR YELLOW
ᚺ	THE UN-EXPECTED	NOT REALLY ONE TO BE USED	9	
ᚾ	CONSTRAINT	FOR SELF-CONTROL OR PROTECTION	10	WHITE or BLUE
ᛁ	IMMOBILITY	FOR A REST PERIOD OR TO STOP SLANDER	11	WHITE or SILVER
ᛃ	YEAR or HEARVEST	FOR JUSTICE OR AGRICULTURE	12	WHITE or GREEN
ᛇ	A CHANNEL	FOR COMMUNICATION WITH OTHER REALMS	13	INDIGO or PURPLE
ᛈ	KARMA HIDDEN FORCE	FOR UNEXPECTED LUCK OR OPPORTUNITY	14	BLUE or GREEN
ᛉ	PROTECTION	FOR PROTECTION AS IN GOING UNNOTICED	15	WHITE
ᛋ	SUN WHEEL	FOR HEALING OR VITAL ENERGY	16	ORANGE, RED or GOLD
ᛏ	VICTORY	FOR VICTORY OR SUCCESS	17	WHITE or GOLD
ᛒ	THE GODDESS	FOR NEW BEGINNINGS TO INVOKE THE GODDESS	18	GREEN or WHITE
ᛖ	HORSE AND RIDER	FOR A SAFE JOURNEY PERFECT FOR A BESOM	19	BLUE
ᛗ	PERFECTED MAN	FOR SELF-IMPROVEMENT, MEDITATION	20	INDIGO or VIOLET
ᛚ	FLUIDITY	TO GAIN INTUITION	21	BLUE or VIOLET
ᛜ	A GOD OF FERTILITY	FOR COMPLETION TO INVOKE THE GOD	22	INDIGO
ᛞ	DAYBREAK	FOR WORKING WHERE TWO WORLDS MEET	23	PALE VIOLET
ᛟ	NOBILITY	TO KNOW ONE'S PLACE IN THE ESTABLISHED ORDER	24	WHITE or GOLD

into a specific number of sections by cutting rings around it. Burn one section a night with appropriate accompanying ritual for a specific number of nights.

Still another way of doing this is to carve a symbolic number of an appropriate rune or sign vertically on a candle, and burn the candle each night so that both the rune and the magically dressed colored wax are consumed by the flame. A traditional number of nights is seven, and these nights should be carefully chosen because the number seven represents a quarter or a phase of the Moon.

Candle magic is a form of Fire magic, and a candle may be seen as a sort of mini-Need Fire. Candle magic is often in the form of a fast charm or spell that needs to be performed in a hurry. Even so, it should be performed within a magically cast Circle, so that the power generated will be contained until it is directed by will at the end of the ritual. It is equally important, or even more so, that candles be dressed, inscribed, and consecrated within a Circle cast in your own tradition and consecrated in the names of the Gods that you are accustomed to.

Candles are usually not entirely consumed as they are used during the year, and these tools that have been anointed and consecrated to the Gods cannot be disposed of with the household trash. Nor is it appropriate to bury these objects of the element of Fire in the element of Earth. Furthermore, they still contain the magic of color, inscribed symbols, anointing oils, and consecration made all the more powerful by ritual use. If possible, it is best to save all ritual candle stumps, sorting them according to color and purpose, and recycle them. We are fortunate to own several antique candle molds that we use for this purpose, but modern tin candle molds are available at many craft shops, and they don't come with the holes, dents, debris, and dead bugs of a century and a half.

Old stumps can be added to new wax, and they will impart their accumulated power to the new candles. Break stumps, remove the old wick, melt the wax in a tin can in a pot of boiling water (a double boiler), and pour it into clean molds that have already been threaded with wick. A spray of Pam down each sleeve will help make the removal of the candles easier, and a dip in ice water will help to set the wax faster.

When an assortment of candle colors have been made, cast your magic Circle, and with your white-handled knife or inscribing tool mark the magic signs on the candles, anoint them with oil, and consecrate them to the Gods and Deities. At this time of the waning solar year, the preparation of magical candles for the year to come is in itself a ritual of Fire that warms and brightens this coldest and darkest month.

A flame, whether a hearth fire or a candle light, has long been used as a focal point for meditation and to induce mediumistic trance, and fire gazing is an ancient form of scrying. At this darkest time of the year, when the spirits of the dead and those that dwell on other planes are closest, it is good to sit before the flame and allow the fire to weave its spell, and if there are any about that wish to communicate, listen for their whispers.

This is a perfect time, too, for nurturing the shamanistic instincts. Seated before a fire (a large white, yellow, or orange candle will do) in a darkened room in which you feel safe and secure, imagine you are in a tiny one-room cabin, a hut in the forest. All that you own and all that you need to survive is contained in this tiny shelter surrounded by seemingly endless dark forest and the creatures that prowl by night. Mentally furnish this room with all your magical tools and only the things that you consider absolutely essential. It is easy, by the flickering light of the fire, as the storm winds of November beat against the windowpanes and the wind howls down the chimney, to visualize the Crone in her forest hut stirring her cauldron hung over the hearth fire, her herbs hung to dry, her cupboard stocked with roots and barks and bones, a crow or toad her only companion. And as she whispers incantations into her cauldron, you lean closer to catch her words and glean her secrets.

It is only one step further back in time to imagine sitting in a small family group knowing not what dangers lurk in darkness just beyond the protective magic Circle of the campfire. As the shifting shadows animate the bison and horses that play across the cave walls, heartbeats quicken to the beat of drums and the shaman's chant. More wood is added to the fire and the smoke ascends into the darkness of the night. Suddenly the pounding stops and we strain to hear the pronouncement of the shaman.

By doing exercises such as these, by hearth fire or by candlelight, it is easy to recognize a different feeling, a feeling of excitement and terror, of primitive magic and ancient mystery that is seldom called for in contemporary life, but one in which the spirit of the Shaman, the Crone, and the Priestess flourish.

As a light snow, perhaps the first of the Winter, dusts the ground and drives the gardener indoors, there are new and different chores to be done. At this time of year the epiphytic cactus from the jungles of Mexico and Central America, popularly known as the Christmas cactus, has set buds and now requires feeding and extra watering if it is to be in full bloom at Yuletide. Its fuchsia or pink blossoms will stand in bright contrast to another Mexican import, the poinsettia, which also needs special attention at this time of year to be in bloom for the holidays.

There are other succulents, too, that are of magical significance. Members of the cactus family, mostly from the American Southwest, all

ASTROLOGICAL SYMBOLS

	PLANETARY SYMBOLS
☉	SUN
☽	MOON
♀	VENUS
♂	MARS
☿	MERCURY
♃	JUPITER
♄	SATURN
♅	URANUS
♆	NEPTUNE
♇	PLUTO

SYMBOL	THE SIGNS OF THE ZODIAC	RULED BY
♈	ARIES	♂
♉	TAURUS	♀
♊	GEMINI	☿
♋	CANCER	☽
♌	LEO	☉
♍	VIRGO	☿
♎	LIBRA	♀
♏	SCORPIO	♇
♐	SAGITTARIUS	♃
♑	CAPRICORN	♄
♒	AQUARIUS	♅
♓	PISCES	♆

bear spines. Some of them bear large and lovely spines arranged in beautiful patterns, and these can be used magically in all the same ways that the thorns of the hawthorn tree are used. Many of these same cacti bloom only at night, and those night-blooming cacti with large white flowers such as the saguaro from Arizona, and the night-blooming cerrus, are of course sacred to the Goddess of the Moon. Epiphytic cacti, those that grow in the branches of trees like the Christmas cactus, have a special affinity for the element of Air. The peyote cactus, which produces buds that are highly narcotic, is one of the herbs that are of importance to the shamans and brujos of Mexico and Central America. A succulent that is a must for the Witch's kitchen, or anyone else's, is the aloe vera. The thick, viscous liquid that can be pressed from its fleshy leaves can bring instant relief to burns, and if applied promptly, liberally, and frequently, the burn will heal without pain or scar. Aloe is also used as a scent in the making of talismans in ceremonial magic and is sacred to Venus.

As the Winter Sun wanes and the Snow Moon waxes full, cast your Circle in the warm glow of candlelight. Salute the Moon in Her snowy whiteness and breathe in the coolness of Her light. Become as still as this Winter night, and know that the activity of the warm light months is behind us. Ahead are the dark months of the year. The Spirit is most active when the body is most still.

November mornings dawn gray and frosted, and deer, brown now in their Winter coats, keep to the edge of the frosted meadow, or race across it not daring to linger, because this is the season of the hunter. One such morning though, dawns with a feeling like no other in the month. As families come together from all parts of the country like some ancient gathering of the clans, as ovens bulge with turkeys and pumpkin pies and TV sets are tuned to parades from Canada and Hawaii, Philadelphia and New York, we all prepare to celebrate a national holiday that is of ancient Pagan origin and has its roots in England.

To celebrate their first harvest of Indian corn, enough to insure a food supply for the coming Winter, the Pilgrims in 1621 held what was then called a Harvest Home. The original Harvest Homes celebrated in England featured the Corn Mother, the representation of the Grain Goddess. It began at Lammas and continued through the entire harvest season until the last crop was in. It featured feasting and drinking to the point that it sometimes interfered with the work of the harvest. By the late sixteenth century it had become the custom not to begin the celebrating until the harvest was complete and the crops were safely in storage.

It is interesting to note that the deeply religious Pilgrims marked this First Thanksgiving not with prayer but with instinctive Pagan feasting and celebration, games and contests, according to the only firsthand account—a letter to England from Edward Winslow. It was not until 1863, when Abraham Lincoln declared the fourth Thursday in November a day of Thanksgiving, that the holiday took on a religious significance.

As we gather around the dinner table with family and friends and bow our heads in silent prayer, it is appropriate that we recall the Pagan origins of this traditional American holiday brought to these shores for us by the Pilgrims, and thank the Gods!

Once Thanksgiving has been celebrated and all thoughts of the harvest are behind us, it is time to look forward to the Winter months ahead, the snow-filled days and the evenings by the fire. The Wheel of the Year is now complete, and it is time to prepare for the next great Sabbat, Yule, when the Wheel of the Year begins again.

AFTERWORD

The Wheel of the Year turns and returns to the point where it began, and every ending is a new beginning. But the Wheel of the Year does not revolve in two-dimensional space. Each new beginning is a little above the one before it, and the Wheel of the Year turns in an ever-rising spiral toward Godhood and the Gods. Each new solar cycle, each new season, each new day, brings us new opportunities to attune ourselves with the rhythms of Nature and the cycle of Her seasons. By the celebration of the Great Sabbats and daily celebration of more subtle changes in Nature, we can become conscious participants in the evolutionary spiral of the universe and thus will truly be living the magical life.

STAY IN TOUCH

On the following pages you will find listed, with their current prices, some of the books and tapes now available on related subjects. Your book dealer stocks most of these, and will stock new titles in the Llewellyn series as they become available. We urge your patronage.

However, to obtain our full catalog, to keep informed of new titles as they are released and to benefit from informative articles and helpful news, you are invited to write for our bi-monthly news magazine/catalog. A sample copy is free, and it will continue coming to you at no cost as long as you are an active mail customer. Or you may keep it coming for a full year with a donation of just $2.00 in U.S.A. ($7.00 for Canada & Mexico, $20.00 overseas, first class mail). Many bookstores also have *The Llewellyn New Times* available to their customers. Ask for it.

Stay in touch! In *The Llewellyn New Times'* pages you will find news and reviews of new books, tapes and services, announcements of meetings and seminars, articles helpful to our readers, news of authors, advertising of products and services, special money-making opportunities, and much more.

The Llewellyn New Times
P.O. Box 64383-Dept. 091, St. Paul, MN 55164-0383, U.S.A.

•   •   •

TO ORDER BOOKS AND TAPES

If your book dealer does not have the books and tapes described on the following pages readily available, you may order them direct from the publisher by sending full price in U.S. funds, plus $2.00 for postage and handling for orders of $10 and under. Orders over $10 will require $3.50 postage and handling. There are no postage and handling charges for orders over $100. UPS Delivery: We ship UPS whenever possible. Delivery guaranteed. Provide your street address as UPS does not deliver to P.O. Boxes. UPS to Canada requires a $50 minimum order. Allow 4-6 weeks for delivery. Orders outside the U.S.A and Canada: Airmail—add $5 per book; add $3 for each non-book item (tapes, etc.); add $1 per item for surface mail.

FOR GROUP STUDY AND PURCHASE

Because there is a great deal of interest in group discussion and study of the subject matter of this book, we feel that we should encourage the adoption and use of this particular book by such groups by offering a special "quantity" price to group leaders or "agents."

Our Special Quantity Price for a minimum order of five copies of *WHEEL OF THE YEAR* is $29.95 Cash-With-Order. This price includes postage and handling within the United States. Minnesota residents must add 6% sales tax. For additional quantities, please order in multiples of five. For Canadian and foreign orders, add postage and handling charges as above. Credit Card (VISA, Master Card, American Express) Orders are accepted. Charge Card Orders only may be phoned free ($15.00 minimum order) within the U.S.A. by dialing 1-800-THE MOON (in Canada call: 1-800-FOR-SELF). Customer Service calls dial 1-612-291-1970. Mail Orders to:

LLEWELLYN PUBLICATIONS
P.O. Box 64383-Dept. 091 / St. Paul, MN 55164-0383, U.S.A.

WICCA: A Guide for the Solitary Practitioner
by Scott Cunningham

Wicca is a book of life, and how to live magically, spiritually, and wholly attuned with Nature. It is a book of sense and common sense, not only about Magick, but about religion and one of the most critical issues of today: how to achieve the much needed and wholesome relationship with our Earth. Cunningham presents Wicca as it is today—a gentle, Earth-oriented religion dedicated to the Goddess and God. This book fulfills a need for a practical guide to solitary Wicca—a need which no previous book has fulfilled.

Here is a positive, practical introduction to the religion of Wicca, designed so that any interested person can learn to practice alone, anywhere in the world. It presents Wicca honestly and clearly, without the pseudo-history that permeates other books. It shows that Wicca is a vital part of twentieth century life.

This book presents the theory and practice of Wicca from an individual's perspective. The section on the Standing Stones Book of Shadows contains solitary rituals for the Esbats and Sabbats. This book, based on the author's nearly two decades of Wiccan practice, presents an eclectic picture of various aspects of this religion. Exercises designed to develop magical proficiency, a self-dedication ritual, herb, crystal and rune magic, recipes for Sabbat feasts, are included.

0-87542-118-0, 240 pgs., 6 x 9, illus., softcover   **$9.95**

THE MAGICAL HOUSEHOLD
by Scott Cunningham and David Harrington

Whether your home is a small apartment or a palatial mansion, you want it to be something special. Now it can be with *The Magical Household*. Learn how to make your home more than just a place to live. Turn it into a place of security, life, fun and magic. Here you will not find the complex magic of the ceremonial magician. Rather, you will learn simple, quick and effective magical spells that use nothing more than common items in your house: furniture, windows, doors, carpet, pets, etc. You will learn to take advantage of the *intrinsic* power and energy that is already in your home, waiting to be tapped. You will learn to make magic a part of your life. The result is a home that is safeguarded from harm and a place which will bring you happiness, health and more.

0-87542-124-5, 208 pgs., illus., softcover   **$7.95**

MAGICAL RITES FROM THE CRYSTAL WELL
by Ed Fitch

In nature, and in the Earth, we look and find beauty. Within ourselves we find a well from which we may draw truth and knowledge. And when we draw from this well, we rediscover that we are all children of the Earth. The simple rites in this book are presented to you as a means of finding your own way back to nature; for discovering and experiencing the beauty and the magic of unity with the source.

These are the celebrations of the seasons: at the same time they are rites by which we attune ourselves to the flow of the force—the energy of life. These are rites of passage by which we celebrate the major transitions we all experience in life.

Here are the Old Ways, but they are also the Ways for Today.

0-87542-230-6, 176 pgs., 7 x 10, illus., softcover.   **$9.95**

BUCKLAND'S COMPLETE BOOK OF WITCHCRAFT
by Raymond Buckland, Ph. D.

Here is the most complete resource to the study and practice of modern, non-denominational Wicca. This is a lavishly illustrated, self-study course for the solitary or group. Included are rituals, exercises for developing psychic talents, and information on all major 'sects' of the Craft, sections on tools, beliefs, dreams, meditations, divination, herbal lore, healing, ritual clothing and much, much more. This book unites theory and practice into a comprehensive course designed to help you develop into a practicing Witch, one of the "Wise Ones." It is written by Dr. Ray Buckland, the very famous and respected authority on witchcraft who first came public with "the Old Religion" in the United States. Large format with workbook-type exercises, profusely illustrated and full of music and chants. Takes you from A to Z in the study of Witchcraft.

Never before has so much information on "the Craft of the Wise" been collected in one place. Traditionally, there are three degrees of advancement in most Wiccan traditions. When you complete studying this book you will be the equivalent of a "Third Degree Witch." Even those who have practiced Wicca for years find useful information in this book, and many covens are using this for their textbook. If you want to become a Witch, or if you merely want to find out what Witchcraft is really about, you will find no better book than this.

0-87542-050-8, 272 pages, 8½ x 11, illus., softcover **$12.95**

IN THE SHADOW OF THE SHAMAN
by Amber Wolfe

Presented in what the author calls a "cookbook shamanism" style, this book shares recipes, ingredients, and methods of preparation for experiencing some very ancient wisdoms—wisdoms of Native American and Wiccan traditions, as well as contributions from other philosophies of Nature, as they are used in the shamanic way. Wolfe encourages us to feel confident and free to use her methods to cook up something new, completely on our own. This blending of ancient formulas and personal methods represents what Ms. Wolfe calls *Aquarian Shamanism*.

Along with increased interest in shamanic ways—the deep, direct ways of Nature—there have also come many people who urge us to follow a certain set method to attune to shamanic energies. In this book you are encouraged to be ever mindful of your truest teacher, the guide within. Wolfe encourages you to follow that wisdom that dwells within your center. When you do this, you are following the heart of the shamanic path; and this makes us open to the wonderful, pure energies of Nature.

In the Shadow of the Shaman is designed to communicate in the most practical, direct ways possible, so that the wisdom and the energy may be shared for the benefit of all. Whatever your system or tradition, you will find this to be a valuable book, a resource, a friend, a gentle guide and support on your journey. Dancing in the shadow of the shaman, you will find new dimensions of Spirit.

0-87542-888-6, 384 pgs., 6 x 9, illus., softcover **$12.95**